BULLSHIT

BULLSHIT

A Good Word and a Vital Part of Leadership

John W Wright

ISBN: 1973740982
ISBN-13: 9781973740988
Library of Congress Control Number: 2017911376
CreateSpace Independent Publishing Platform
North Charleston, South Carolina

CONTENTS

Preface

THERE COULD BE a number of reasons why you picked up this book and are reading this preface. I would hope that the first reason is you think it's preposterous that someone thinks bullshit is a vital part of leadership. Actually, it's important for me that you are thinking along those lines, because it means there is an entire world out there where you can think about leadership in a different, important way…a breakthrough way.

Second, you, like me, might simply like the word *bullshit*, use it often, and find it interesting to explore a book on this rather amazing word.

The vast majority of people think of and use the word *bullshit* to connect it to exaggeration, stretching the truth, lying, and so on. We don't think of the word as connected to motivating, inspiring, and challenging people to go further than they ever thought they could go. That is what the second half of this book is about. I will make a case that positive bullshit without question is a vital part of leadership, and the best leaders in the world understand this and know how to use it.

Before we do that, in chapters 1 through 5, we are going to explore some of my thoughts on the word itself. I have been involved in leadership my entire life as a college and NFL athlete and through thirty-five years in the corporate world. From the twin-city college towns of Champaign–Urbana in central Illinois, I have been one of the top developers of field leaders in one of the highest-ranked, most respected companies in the world: Northwestern Mutual. I have always felt that for people to focus on something, they need to relax first, which is why I adhere to the philosophy that "focus follows fun." So before we focus on leadership and its connection to positive bullshit, we are going to have some fun with the word and learn how rather amazing and special it is.

Think for a moment about the world of athletics. Pick your sport: football, lacrosse, soccer, baseball, basketball, or whatever, where thousands of people (many times, a hundred thousand people) can be heard chanting one special word, and that word is bullshit… bullshit…bullshit. This obviously happens when the frenzied fans are frustrated and upset with the referee's call on a specific play. They want the ref to understand their displeasure and would love for him or her to change the "bad" call to a "good" call, or at least make more "good" calls in the future. Why is no other word used in these chants? What makes bullshit so special? That's one of the reasons I wrote this book.

Every day in our lives, our minds make the "wrong" call, and it needs to be overturned. Overturning a "bad" call in our minds isn't an easy or simple thing to do, so many times, we need to bullshit ourselves or those we lead to get this done. As hard as this might be for you to agree with or believe at this moment, by the time you have finished this short book, I feel confident you will agree, and that's my no-bullshit promise to you.

INTRODUCTION

IT'S BEEN SAID that words create worlds. While that statement is meaningful, I'm not sure it's a true north
concept—it may be just partly correct (meaning it's not
quite complete, for words can only create worlds if they're
acted upon). We all know how to live a perfect life. The
problem isn't knowing, it's doing. It's acting.

The first part of this book is an exploration of one
very special word. It's a word that most people on the
planet use no matter what language they speak. It's also a
word we use to communicate many different things. If we
lived in this world alone or on a desert island, we wouldn't
need this discussion. But we don't. Living and connecting
with others is vital to our existence. So, for us to grow and
prosper, we need to improve how we connect—not only
with others, but with ourselves.

Most creatures on this amazing planet of ours, including human beings, live in groups. Migratory birds—
geese, ducks, doves, and the like—live in flocks. Quail live
together in coveys, ants live in colonies, bees in hives, and

insects in swarms. Lions live in prides, wolves in packs, buffalo in herds, and human beings (who, we'd like to think, rule this planet) live in tribes.

For a number of reasons, this togetherness, this community living, causes and requires us to communicate with one another, which we accomplish in two primary ways.

Our number one means of communication is body language. It's also the first way most living creatures communicate. To take a piece from Robert Cooper's outstanding book *Get Out of Your Own Way*, spoken language is a recent development in human history, emerging only about five thousand years ago, so the brain has a great, enduring capacity to work with nonverbal signals. By some accounts, at least 80 percent of human communication is nonverbal. You clearly know a mother bear is upset with you when she charges to protect her cubs versus how happy she is when eating her salmon lunch on the shore of a pristine river. You know the difference between your dog's wagging tail and the excitement and love she shows versus the bared fangs of a guard dog ready to lunge. It's easy to tell the difference between a lioness stalking her prey and one stretched out taking a nap.

Human beings also communicate through body language—something that's extremely hard to fake. A horse can read human body language and know exactly the extent of your riding experience when you mount up simply by how you feel to him when you sit on his back. If you're an inexperienced rider, you'll be wise not to mount a spirited horse because the horse will know in that first instant that he can take you for a ride instead of vice versa.

If you doubt me, just ask all-world guy and all-pro cornerback for the Chicago Bears and Carolina Panthers, NFL's 2014 Man of the Year, Charles "Peanut" Tillman, about his wild ride down a beautiful Costa Rican beach on a horse that clearly understood Peanut's lack of riding experience! Body language never whispers; it always screams.

Jury consultants rely heavily on body language in advising attorney clients. Corporate executives read body language when they interview prospective hires. Police officers' lives often depend on their ability to read the body language of someone they confront, and a coach can tell if his or her team is ready to play by the way the members walk out of the locker room and warm up prior to the game. Almost without fail, body language trumps our second means of communication, which is words.

Just as the animal kingdom uses sounds to communicate, we have our own sounds, which we've crafted into words. In fact, most of us consider words our principal means of communication with others. It's true that words are very important. Words do create worlds, or as I said earlier, they definitely can, provided we act on them.

The first section of this book will be about just one word—a word used by most people but understood by all. A word that can bring an audience to laughter but send your child to the principal's office. A word that for many people has negative connotations—false statements, lying, exaggerating, or nonsense. Yet it's a powerful word, a single utterance that eliminates the need for a bunch of words to convey a pointed meaning.

I'll make a case that this word also has a positive side: a redeeming quality that can be used to make us better and help us grow. Could this one amazing little word actually be a vital element in leadership? My answer to that question is a definite "Yes!" What is this all-powerful word we're about to explore? It's bullshit!

Now, I didn't wake up one day and just decide to write a book on bullshit. The inspiration for the title, *Bullshit—A Good Word and A Vital Part of Leadership,* came to me after watching *On Golden Pond,* a popular film from the early 1980s, which I'll say more about later.

But the "why" behind the book is really what catapulted this concept to the forefront of my teaching. In the spring of 1999, I was preparing a speech for the executive offices and field leadership of Northwestern Mutual, one of the best respected and most highly rated financial services companies in the world. To really push the envelope, I decided to entitle my presentation "Is Bullshit a Part of Leadership?"

In my career as a professional athlete in the NFL and a corporate executive for many years thereafter, I've delivered hundreds of speeches, yet none were as widely accepted or enjoyed as much as this presentation on bullshit as part of leadership. The audience's overwhelming approval truly stunned me. By the time I finished, they had tears of laughter in their eyes, and afterward, they smothered me with accolades, e-mails, phone calls, and letters. One very successful attendee, Bill Hornsby, even sent me a decorative pillow embroidered with this message:

> *If you can't dazzle them with brilliance,*
> *baffle them with bullshit.*

Of course, we're talking here about positive bullshit. They hadn't thought about it before, but my presentation must have struck a harmonious note within. Clearly, it was something people in their positions should have been thinking and acting upon. I saw that I'd struck a chord of acceptance with powerful and successful men and women in the business world. After this experience, I also saw that positive bullshit was such a special and exciting concept that not only should it be discussed further, it should be implemented and celebrated as a skill and trait for leaders and team builders.

Focus follows fun, so let's have a little fun with this amazing word, bullshit.

PART I

BULLSHIT—A GOOD WORD

CHAPTER 1

BULLSHIT THOUGHTS

FROM THIS POINT forward, I'll be defining and referring to bullshit in three different and distinct ways: exaggerated bullshit (EBS), negative bullshit (NBS), and positive bullshit. This third version, we'll be calling PBS, or +BS—not to be confused with PBS, the Public Broadcasting Service (an organization my wife and I love, which, at different times during its broadcasts, actually deals in all three forms: EBS, NBS, and +BS).

I have no idea what you may be saying or thinking to yourself as you read this—possibly, "Wow, a book on bullshit!" You probably won't read many academic publications or other treatises on the topic. It won't appear in history books, and most leading coaching and leadership experts probably haven't incorporated bullshit into their books, programs, or teaching methods. Even if they have, they may not know it by that name or recognize its power.

In my opinion, that's a bunch of bullshit in and of itself. As a former NFL player, business leader, coach, and mentor, the manner in which I teach has been grounded in out-of-the-box thinking. I believe much of my success in mentoring so many leaders has been directly related to my ability to understand and deal with EBS and NBS quickly and effectively and to use the concept of +BS as an effective leadership and training tool. Great leaders recognize, avoid, and deal with EBS and NBS, while they're masters at using +BS to motivate and lead individuals and teams to greater success.

Good leaders and coaches motivate their players and teams to be better. Great leaders and coaches motivate their players and teams to be better than they *think* they can be, and this takes skill in being able to use +BS.

Just think about some of the best-known promises of the last one hundred years: to win two world wars, to put a man on the moon, to move forward after such an unthinkable tragedy as 9/11, and to stop the spread of horrendous and often fatal diseases. These promises have been met while we have yet to fulfill others: put an end to world hunger, defeat terrorism, and eliminate homelessness and unemployment.

Many people have stood in front of national and even international audiences and made some +BS promises, a few even promising to predict a Super Bowl victory! +BS helps us move beyond recognizing the problem and closer to the solution. Most meaningful changes have started with a goal laced with a little bit—sometimes a lot—of +BS. Each of the monumental assurances mentioned above was made with one part hope and one part fact and was underwritten with +BS. We weren't entirely sure we could put a man on the moon, win that war, or find a cure for a terrible disease. But we told ourselves we could, and we have, mostly because one or many brave souls seized the opportunity to inspire and motivate a team, town, region, or country to support the cause and move collectively toward the ultimate goal.

It's a fact that +BS is a way to motivate ourselves into believing anything is possible, even against all odds. It's a way to inspire and move ourselves and others to action when inaction would simply mean maintaining an unacceptable status quo. Consider this contrast: we use EBS and NBS to call others out on their dishonesty and inconsistency, while +BS can give hope to those who desperately need it. So I hope you'll believe me that bullshit is a good word if it is used to help leaders, coaches, and team builders create a little bit of fun and a lot of forward movement.

To climb higher on the ladder of success, to cross the River of Resistance into our unlived lives, to be green and growing versus ripe and rotting, we need to change something we're doing, and change is difficult. Great leaders understand this and are effective at doing whatever it takes to enable those whom they lead to see and act on their vision for change.

You may have to use +BS to move others from where they are to where they need to be or to persuade an underdog to buy into your mission. To reach amazing levels of success yourself and to set aside fears, limitations, and boundaries, you may have to avoid or cut through NBS or EBS at the same time as you're increasing your skillful use of +BS.

However you decide to use bullshit, this book will help you better understand and implement the concept into your life and your goals. The approach is unique, different, and creative. The best kind of bullshit, +BS, is an avenue to bigger ideas, greater dedication, and an undying determination to inspire, motivate, and excite people to move not just *toward* their goals but *to* and *through* their goals.

Great journeys require great guides! These guides lead us to where we want to go, and, more importantly, they inspire and motivate us to go further than we thought we could go. My hope is that this book will serve as a guide for you on the rest of your journey through life.

CHAPTER 2

WHY BULLSHIT IS A GOOD WORD

As I've said, my inspiration for the title of this book came from a 1981 movie, *On Golden Pond*, based on Ernest Thompson's play of the same name. Directed by Mark Rydell, the film starred Katharine Hepburn, Henry Fonda, Dabney Coleman, Jane Fonda, and Doug McKeon.

On Golden Pond tells the story of Norman Thayer, a retired professor who's frustrated by the world he and his loving wife, Ethel, live in. They've owned a summer cottage on Golden Pond since early in their long marriage. This particular summer, their daughter Chelsea, whom they haven't seen for years, feels the need to be there for Norman's eightieth birthday. She and her fiancé will be on their way to Europe the next day, and they drop in, not only to celebrate, but to enlist Norman and Ethel to care for Chelsea's future stepson, Billy, while they're gone. As it opens, *On Golden Pond* portrays the Thayer family's entertaining, credible, and heartfelt dynamic.

Norman is a grumpy, sarcastic, complaining old man with a bark much louder than his bite. He loves his wife Ethel dearly, and she's clearly the center of his world. Their daughter Chelsea has always had issues with her father, and their relationship is still stretched to the limit when she returns with her fiancé, a successful dentist, and his son, Billy Ray. Billy is a teenager with a short attention span who is easily bored and difficult to entertain. Norman doesn't want to be responsible for the boy, but eventually, Ethel persuades him that they must accept the challenge to "entertain" Billy for the summer.

As the younger couple is about to leave for Europe, father Bill shows very little emotion toward his son and doesn't even hug the boy to say goodbye. Rather, he remarks coldly, "You gonna be OK now?"

With little sincerity or care for his dad's comment, Billy Ray's response is passive. "Oh sure."

Bill then says, "Behave yourself," with Billy retorting, "You guys behave yourself too."

Chelsea goes to Billy and gives him a kiss, saying only, "Goodbye, kid." And with that, they leave for the airport. As the car disappears into the woods, Billy throws a half-hearted wave in their direction, then faces Norman and Ethel. With his true pain shining through, he speaks harshly. "Just want you guys to know I'm not about to take any crap from you."

This statement clearly shocks them both, but rather than respond, they simply gather their emotions and head for the cabin, gearing up for what could be some frustrating and long days to come.

As they walk away, they leave Billy crying, angry, and frustrated. The reality sets in that once again, he's been dumped by his father. To cope with his disappointment, he begins angrily throwing pinecones into the forest.

But Ethel, striding eloquently, attempts to cut the negativity. "Well, gentlemen," she says, "it's a beautiful day. We're going fishing."

Taken by surprise, something he rarely welcomes, Norman says, "What? We're going what?"

"Fishing," Ethel tells him. "You remember fishing, Norman. You're going to show Billy what life is all about on Golden Pond. Come on, Billy."

Hearing this, Billy rolls his eyes as he throws another pinecone into the forest, barking out an angry "Bullshit!"

Taken aback, Ethel says, "I beg your pardon. Does that mean you can't wait to get out there, or it's not your cup of tea?"

Billy reinforces his earlier remark. "It's bullshit, that's all."

Maintaining her usual clear-headed grace, Ethel says, "Well, I see. Come on Norman, let's get ready."

And with that, she calmly strolls into the house and leaves Norman, the seemingly out-of-touch old man, to consider how to handle this otherwise troubled youth who's obviously challenging the older couple's authority over him.

At that point, with all the sincerity he can muster, Norman says, "You like that word, don't you, bullshit?"

A defiant Billy turns to look at Norman. "Yeah."

Norman hears him, gathers his thoughts while looking the young man straight in the eye, then responds. "It's a good word."

With that one simple but sweeping statement, Norman transcends boundaries, bridges gaps in both age and life, and connects to an otherwise disconnected young man. His heartfelt statement breaks the ice and helps him begin to build a bond with the boy. By the film's end, Norman and young Billy seem more like grandfather and grandson than the strangers they were just days before.

When Norman delivers his four-word response, "It's a good word," to Billy, he connects with this young teenager probably better than anyone in Billy's life has up to that time. He communicates to Billy that he understands his pain, understands how his father treats him, and understands how he feels. In that moment, he reaches the boy. When Billy meant to let Norman know exactly how he felt, few words in his vocabulary could have been used more appropriately or had more impact than his single word, bullshit.

For me, that scene speaks volumes to the power of the concept of bullshit. After watching that special moment in cinema history and replaying it often later in my mind, I came to realize that this simple yet often-used word is more than just a word. It can be a concept, an expression, an icebreaker, a crowd pleaser, a motivator, a stimulus, a defense mechanism, a vantage point, a leadership tool, and a big-time idea for us to explore together.

It's true that the seed for this book was planted in my mind by that special scene in *On Golden Pond*. Since then, the nourishment that helped this small seed grow into something more meaningful didn't occur in a theater or in front of the television. It actually occurred as I saw people around me respond to the lessons I offered surrounding the concept of +BS. My subsequent journey has included coming to terms with and understanding exactly how much value and meaning the word bullshit actually has.

In fact, I see it everywhere. I see it in the actions, decisions, and behaviors of leaders, team builders, CEOs, coaches, politicians, doctors, lawyers, and almost every other profession in the world. We all love some good, old-fashioned bullshit. Bullshit is an everyday word for an everyday man or woman. It's part of the glue that holds us together, even if we don't always recognize its presence.

But why should you care? Well, I'm confident I can show you the "why" in the pages that follow. That's my responsibility and my promise to you. I intend to work diligently to demonstrate the enormous value you can find in using +BS to motivate others, avoid difficult situations, and call people out when they're full of shit. Together, we'll dive deep into the concept and break it down to its most fundamental pieces. And once we've done that, my hope is that you'll agree that bullshit isn't a good word, it's actually a *great* word.

CHAPTER 3

THE ORIGINS OF BULLSHIT

CURIOUSLY, THE ORIGINS of a word like bullshit, so ingrained in our culture, have quite an unclear history. Having said that, let's dive into what my research uncovered about where this amazing word arose and the myriad uses it has found.

Obviously, bullshit is a combination of two words: *bull* and *shit*. Let's begin with the first one, *bull*. When we hear this word, most of us connect it to the male bovine animal, capable of reproduction. We all envision a big, burly, beefy critter, perhaps with horns or perhaps without, possibly with a ring through its nose, breathing heavily or even snorting, and with an extremely nasty and unpredictable temperament.

If you look up synonyms for the word *bull*, you find such words as balderdash, baloney, bilge, bunkum, claptrap, crap, hogwash, rubbish, and trash. Isn't it interesting how such a magnificent, imposing creature as a mature bull gets connected to so many adjectives that describe undesirable human traits? With that said, most people would concede that, on its own, the word *bull* has collected negative connotations.

Bull may also be applied to settings for relaxed communication, such as "bull session" and "shooting the bull." You might think that bull means very little when actually it can mean a great deal. Both these expressions describe a coming together, catching up, shooting the breeze, and exchanging information. So when we consider its proper place in the English language, we can't undervalue or underestimate this good old word. But we can't stop there, having dealt with only half of this vital marriage in semantics.

Both the history and the evolution in usage of *shit* are even more fascinating. It is one of those special words that truly transcends boundaries. It is for the young and the old, the weak and the strong, the rich and the poor, and for cable television and the big screen. It can be a noun, an adjective, and, perhaps most importantly, a verb. Though the more prudish among us may not readily admit it, *shit* is, in fact, one of the most widely used English words. A respectable physician I know told me he had no idea ladies used the word until the first time he made his well-brought-up bride mad.

"Shit": we say it when we're happy, sad, frustrated, elated, mad, and annoyed. One dictionary lists ninety various uses for the word: shit a brick, shit a shitter, shit bullets, shit creek, shit happens, and on and on. Even with all that said, historically speaking, it's not crystal clear where and why we began using this word in such creative ways. However, my research did turn up one seemingly logical and historically interesting story about its origins.

During the seventeenth through nineteenth centuries, the English ruled the seas and much of the globe. They shipped goods all over the populated world and were considered to be the elite of the merchant marines. Their ships carried a wide range of goods and products, one of which, interestingly enough, was cow manure. Highly valued, it was considered the most nourishing fertilizer known at that time.

Before it was shipped, the manure was first dried, then formed into large bales for storage deep in the ships' hulls. During the voyage, however, waves would often come across the decks of these small trading vessels, and if they worked their way down to the lowest level of the ship, the manure got wet. And, once the previously inoffensive dried manure was thoroughly soaked, it took on an entirely different chemical form.

Wet manure produces methane gas, which is explosive. Anyone who's ever lit a candle to counteract bathroom odors knows the match will flare up with considerable smoke, burning off gas produced by healthy human digestion. For those of you who've ventured into a more advanced investigation of burning human gas, we only have to remind you of those camping trips with your buddies or a few late-night fraternity get-togethers where you might have experienced lighting a fart and seen a six-inch flame rocket out of your or someone else's ass!

And so, the story goes, the first time a seaman with a lantern ventured deep into the hull of a ship where bales of now-wet manure were producing large quantities of methane gas, the minute he lit his lantern, you guessed it. *Boom!* The huge explosion caused major damage to the ship's hull.

Now, it's well known that among wide-roaming sailors, word travels fast. Seamen all across the world soon learned a valuable lesson—so valuable, in fact, that they told the sea captains they had to change the way they stored manure shipments to keep it dry. And so, thereafter, before the bales of dried manure were carried on board, the captains had the dockworkers mark them with the words "Ship High in Transit." As you might imagine, before long the dockworkers began shortening those four words to just four letters—*SHIT.* How amazing is that? Shit is actually an acronym! And thus the word *shit* was born.

There's something so fascinating about this word that it's hard to tear ourselves away from exploring it. *The Urban Dictionary* describes it as "one of the most popular swear/cuss/curse words/profanities." But that doesn't come close to cataloguing all of its charms. As *New York Times* best-selling author David Sedaris wrote,

"Shit is the tofu of cursing and can be molded to whichever condition the speaker desires."

Furthermore, its uses go far beyond cursing. Without question, shit ranks right up there as one of the most functional words in the English language. You can get shit-faced, be shit out of luck, or have shit for brains. With a little effort, you can get your shit together, find a place for your shit, or be asked to shit or get off the pot. You can smoke shit, buy shit, lose shit, find shit, forget shit, and tell others to eat shit. Some people know their shit, while others can't tell the difference between shit and Shinola.

There are lucky shits, dumb shits, and crazy shits. There's bullshit, horse shit, chicken shit, dog shit, ape shit, bat shit, and jack shit. You can throw shit, sling shit, catch shit, shoot the shit, or duck when shit hits the fan. You can give a shit, or you can serve shit on a shingle. You can find yourself in deep shit or be happier than a pig in shit. Some days are colder than shit, some days are hotter than shit, and some days are just plain shitty.

Some music sounds like shit, things can look like shit, and there are times when you feel like shit. You can have too much shit, not enough shit, the right shit, the wrong shit, or a lot of weird shit. You can carry shit, have a mountain of shit, or find yourself up shit's creek without a paddle. Sometimes, everything you touch turns to shit, while at other times, you may fall into a bucket of shit and come out smelling like a rose. When you take time to give it due consideration, you can see that shit is one of the basic building blocks of the English language. By now, you get the point. Even more important, once you know your shit, you don't need to know anything else!

And, at some point in the forgotten mists of time, some scholar or learned individual decided to marry the well-known animal with its by-product, coupling this amazing word *shit* with *bull* and thereby providing me with a working premise for my book.

And that's no bullshit.

If you'd like to dig even deeper into the history of the word bullshit, you may want to read Harry Frankfurt's wonderful little book, *On Bullshit*, published in 2005. Frankfurt is an emeritus professor of philosophy at Princeton University, and his little treatise has given many readers considerable joy.

CHAPTER 4

THE BIG FIVE

ANY DISCUSSION ON the word bullshit would not be complete without mentioning some of the other most popular animal shits that we effectively use in our language.

In many circles, five is a special number, as it is to the head men's basketball coach at Duke University, Mike Krzyzewski. I once heard Coach Z give a talk in which he said he likes the number five for a couple of reasons. First, a basketball team has five players, which is certainly meaningful for him. Second, he likes listing five things during a speech, because five fingers form a fist, and a fist packs far more power than four or three fingers.

Five is also a special number for those who hunt big game in Africa, as five special animals constitute big-game hunting's hall of fame. (In case you're interested, those five are the elephant, rhino, Cape buffalo, lion, and leopard.) Five is a favorite number of mine, as it was my son's number when he played football for the University of Illinois. So, with all that in mind, I decided to discuss with you my list of the big five in the animal feces world.

1. YOUR PERSONAL FAVORITE

I said in the preface of this book that one might think it preposterous that I claim that bullshit is a vital part of leadership. What I'm about to propose might seem even more preposterous than the leadership discussion: that you actually have a favorite animal shit, which makes your day when you run across it. If you are an outdoors person or a hunter, you totally understand where I'm going with this favorite animal shit thought. Yet I'm confident most of you have never thought about such a thing, not even once in your life. If that's so, if you've never given this subject any thought or, worse yet, you lack the knowledge even to make a selection, I'm afraid you may have missed one of the great joys of life. It's time to remedy that deficiency, so let us get to the big five animal shits. Some education along the way is called for, which I'll be glad to provide as we go.

I know, most of you reading this book are already saying, "Are you kidding, John? I don't have a favorite animal shit! Why would I even want such a thing?"

If that's the case, you may need to sharpen your awareness when exploring the great outdoors. Your number one selection should be the animal shit that excites you when you come across it in the wild. My guess is that most Americans have never spent time thinking about it or have never even seen a reason to do so. And that's a shame I hope to remedy. In my opinion, it's time you took a bigger bite out of life.

Scatology is the science and study of animal feces, and if that's your profession, you're called a scatologist. Yes, believe it or not, there are people who devote their educational and professional lives to becoming experts in all types of scat, feces, crap, poop, dung, shit, or whatever you want to call it. And if you happen to be among the millions of Americans who love, enjoy, and spend time in the outdoors, you know the excitement of happening upon your favorite animal scat. Most naturalists, while they may not have a degree in scatology, are proficient at recognizing various types of animal scat in the wild.

If you hunt, you'd better know how to recognize the feces of your prey. The most widely hunted big-game animal in the United States is the white-tailed deer, and, believe me, in any area where they plan to hunt, all deer hunters get excited to discover fresh "field raisins," as they affectionately call deer droppings.

This ability to recognize animal scat is something you should never pooh-pooh. The hiker in one of our beautiful national parks in the Great West understands the extreme importance of recognizing fresh grizzly-bear scat and knows that clearing the area might be a lifesaving move. Yet someone who's there to hunt the grizzly bear is overjoyed to come upon a steaming pile of fresh bear scat, which indicates their prey is close at hand.

Every hunter clearly understands what I mean. I was sharing this thought with a good buddy of mine from Dallas, Texas, an extremely successful CEO and a big-time big-game hunter, Tait Cruse. He related a true story about a hunt he was on in Africa, pursuing the largest of all African antelope, the kudu. Having trouble finding the animal they were after, his trackers decided they needed the services of the best tracker in their village. So, with a little financial incentive from Tait, they convinced the man to join the hunt and quickly got on the trail of the kudu they wanted. When they came upon kudu feces, the expert tracker picked some up, took a big bite, and proclaimed that the kudu was twenty minutes ahead of them. Now that is *really* taking a bite out of life, what I call a serious love of the hunt. I was sharing this rather amazing story with a close friend of mine, Kevin Spahn, who is also a friend of Tait's. Kevin is one of the most respected wealth advisors with the Northwestern Mutual, which is why he knows Tait so well. A big part of the reason Tait and Kevin are such powerful leaders is because they so clearly understand that positive bullshit is a vital part of leadership. Both, can REALLY "spin a yarn" so to speak. That is why when Kevin heard this story his first comment was "That's bullshit" ...obviously referring to EBS, which is exaggerated bullshit. I reassured Kevin, that as much as the story might seem to be EBS...it's 100% accurate. It might even be where the expression "eat shit" arose.

While the nonhunters among you may not relate, you can still take the opportunity to choose your own favorite animal feces to start off our special big five list. Speaking personally, mine is quail scat. My father and grandfather were ardent quail hunters, and my father raised and trained bird dogs

22

and had me hunting quail by the time I was nine years old. I fell in love with this sport and have been training dogs and hunting quail now for more than sixty-two years. My lifelong quail hunting partners, son Johnny, Maurie Daigneau from Milwaukee, Wisconsin, and Mike Maroney from Denver, Colorado, all would agree with what I'm about to share.

One very exciting moment in quail hunting is discovering a quail roost. Quail live in groups called coveys, comprising from two or three to as many as thirty birds or more. At night, they sleep in a perfect circle, tails together in the center and heads facing out. This habit serves a dual purpose, both keeping them warm and allowing them to fly up all at once if an enemy threatens. Discovering a fresh quail roost is a sure sign of a covey of quail nearby, and believe me, that is very exciting.

A lifelong friend of mine was Ed Patridge, a successful bank executive from Alabama. I was blessed to be one of Ed's hunting partners, along with Joe Whitt, former Auburn University football coach and now a retired Auburn Associate Athletic Director. When we were in the field, we both loved hearing Ed discover a quail roost and shout out in his Alabama drawl, "Quail roost! Where there's a turd, there's a bird!" So for me, without hesitation, my number-one animal shit of the big five is quail shit.

One last comment about your personal favorite: don't be disappointed or overly distraught if you don't currently have a favorite animal shit, for you still have time to create a fuller life!

2. DOG SHIT

Beyond your personal favorite, most people in America, unless you have been living under a rock, are familiar with dog shit, since dogs have a strong hold on the position of the second favorite US pet. According to the American Pet Products Association survey of 2015–2016, there are 77,800,000 dogs and 88,800,000 cats in the United States. If we take the number of dogs and multiply by an average eight ounces of manure each dog produces every day, we come up with an incredible 38,900,000 pounds of dog shit deposited by man's best friend daily. That's a staggering amount to pick up, clean up, wash up, and step in every twenty-four hours. I doubt anyone will argue the significance and influence of that number in our lives. Yet, with that said, dog shit may be the least prominent shit among the big four (dog, chicken, horse, and bull) applied to human actions. When and if we tie it to human behavior, it usually has to do with poor performance, such as, "Our team played like dog shit today."

This is a very important distinction, because none of its other uses are abstract. Frequent uses of "dog shit" include the following: "Be careful of the dog shit," "don't step in the dog shit," "watch out—there's some dog shit in the yard," and the one we all hate: "I just stepped in some dog shit." Is there anything more frustrating than getting into your new Mercedes to catch the unforgettable essence of dog shit? Knowing that the dog shit that was once in your yard is now on your feet and the carpet of your new car is not a good way to start the day.

With very little trouble, most of us can recall our worst stepping-in-dog-shit event. Mine is permanently etched in my mind. My wife and I live on an eighty-acre property, which I call a ranch, because I think it sounds more adventuresome than a farm. We have ten dogs, five barn cats, and three horses. As I've said, I train bird dogs for my quail-hunting activities.

A few of the dogs get to come in the house on a regular basis, one being our very old yellow lab, Chief. Now it's a fact that dogs in advanced age, like human beings, start to lose control of some bodily functions. On the evening I have in mind, Chief had been in the house for much of the day. One of my nightly missions is to lock up the house on the way to bed, and for whatever reason, on this night I was barefoot. Well, you guessed it. The lights in the foyer were off as I made my way toward the front door. The centerpiece of that foyer is a beautiful Oriental rug, and that night, waiting for me in the dark in the middle of that rug, was a fresh pile of dog shit, courtesy of good ol' Chief. My bare foot completed a direct hit. If you've ever felt warm dog shit ooze through your toes, you won't forget it.

My initial outburst, muffled to keep my wife from knowing what had happened, was "SHIT!" It took me quite a while to first, get my foot cleaned up, then the rug, and I mean *really* cleaned up. I treated it like the scrub down of a murder scene. My wife would not have been a happy camper knowing that Chief had added his unique patch of color to her Oriental. Once I had everything cleaned up, leaving absolutely no evidence or odor, I went on to bed.

In the morning, I briefly debated keeping the knowledge of what had happened to myself, but after finding absolutely no stain, evidence, or smell of the mishap (which, incidentally, shows the amazing resilience of Oriental rugs), I decided to share the news that I'd stepped in some of Chief's dog shit the night before. So I did, nicely, and I'm glad to report that Chief and I are both still alive.

Here's my point. If we owned cattle, which we don't, and if we kept a few special cattle in the house, which probably wouldn't be smart, and if one of those cattle was a bull who happened to shit in the foyer, I would never have told my wife, "I stepped in some bullshit last night." It just wouldn't fit. And my wife would be the first to say that in our long, wonderful marriage, I've often piled our home high with tons of my bullshit.

3. CHICKEN SHIT

This term, too, has multiple uses and meanings. First, chicken shit can be used appropriately to refer to a chicken's digestive product. If you were collecting eggs from the ol' chicken coop, it would be totally accept-able to tell anyone willing to listen, "There's a lot of chicken shit in the coop."

Today, more people than ever are able to recognize chicken shit. We're seeing an interesting societal phe-nomenon that chickens, and the inevitable chicken shit, are quite in style. Any feed-store owner has a number of customers, members of their community elite, who keep chickens. This chicken mania has even touched my fam-ily. My son and daughter-in-law live in Atlanta's Buckhead neighborhood, one of the top five (there's that number again) most influential zip codes in the United States. And yep, Laura raises chickens, treating them more like pets than the egg-laying machines they have become. I suspect she has a much clearer understanding of chicken shit today than she ever dreamed she'd have.

But chicken shit can also refer to certain human ac-tions that have nothing to do with scat. Let's look at an ex-ample. Suppose you're in a very important meeting with the president of a company and some key employees. The president describes a new program he wants to initiate to deal more effectively with employees, then asks for feed-back from the group. Bob is the human resources special-ist, yet he and most of the others in the room view this new program as the wrong way to go. Not a soul speaks up, particularly not Bob. Later, when the attendees dis-cuss the meeting among themselves, it would be fair and appropriate to say, as someone may have done, "Not giving the president his real opinion was a chicken-shit move on Bob's part."

This hypothetical case is actually very real. I often talk with CEOs of powerful, successful, highly ranked Fortune 100 companies, and in one such discussion, a CEO related the exact story I've used to describe Bob's behavior—a meeting where the president wanted feedback on an issue on the table. When no one voiced a negative response, the CEO said, "If we're all in agreement, then let's go ahead with the new plan." Immediately afterward, one executive who hadn't spoken up in the meeting told the CEO privately, "This proposal isn't going to work." Here's a perfect example of how a senior officer's chicken-shit behavior can cause real problems. The CEO found his subordinate's after-the-meeting comment extremely frustrating. In some way, shape, or form, chicken-shit actions or nonactions usually derive from a lack of courage—an important topic we'll talk more about later.

4. HORSE SHIT

This one, too, has dual meanings: equine manure and human behavior. It's quite reasonable to say, "There's a lot of horse shit out there in the corral." On the other hand, the same term can apply to human beings' actions. Suppose our same president from the example above decides to withhold the bonuses he'd earlier promised, coming up with some lame excuse about why it won't happen. In this instance, saying "What a horse-shit move!" would be appropriate. Both number three, chicken shit, and number four, horse shit, have definite and important applications for human actions that, in certain situations, may even be a better fit than bullshit.

5. BULLSHIT

Without question, bullshit seems to be the quintessential animal-shit name. It's interesting to note that bullshit is one word, when all the other animal shits are two separate words. Chicken shit, horse shit, dog shit, and quail shit, with the millions of other animal shits, also require two words, and we don't know why.

Unique in another way, bullshit is hardly ever used now to describe the actual feces of the male bovine animal. It just doesn't fit if you're walking in a cow pasture, hit a land mine of manure, and say, "Hey, I just stepped in some bullshit." After many years of use, misuse, and abuse, bullshit, having finally come to denote only human actions, truly deserves the special place it holds in our language.

No discussion of animal shits describing human actions would be complete without mentioning three more, yet less used players. Bat shit, jack shit, and ape shit. Both bat shit and ape shit can be deftly used to describe unusual, or "crazy" actions of humans. "He simply went bat shit." We pull in jack shit when we want to describe a lack of knowledge or intelligence as "he doesn't know jack shit."

Now that we've had some fun with word play, I hope, after our exhaustive study, that you're ready to explore with me the vast possibilities +BS has to offer in the realm of leadership. By taking the trouble to acquire skill in its application, you'll begin to see bullshit in a completely different light—one that is bright and lucid and that builds championship teams, elevates leaders, and pushes the boundaries of success. Together, we can share in this enlightening and exciting journey, using the concept of +BS to unlock old habits and foster a far richer approach to life.

PART II

LEADERSHIP–PUTTING POSITIVE BULLSHIT TO WORK

CHAPTER 5

A NATIONAL CHAMPIONSHIP

As you know, the book's title is *Bullshit—A Good Word and A Vital Part of Leadership.* We have now spent enough time on why bullshit is a good word, and I hope it may have brought a smile to your face. The remaining pages are the why behind this book and a chance for me to share my fervent belief that positive bullshit is truly a *vital* part of leadership, whether leading yourself or others.

I'll kick it off with a true story about a strong leader who touched the life of a young man. It's an account of a coach and an athlete, and it's about how losing turned into winning. The coach was my father, Robert C. Wright, and the athlete was a track star named Charlton Ehizuelen. It was May 1974 at the NCAA Track and Field Championships, which were held at the University of Texas in Austin.

My father was then head track coach for the University of Illinois, the "Fighting Illini." He had built a strong team that included this young Nigerian, who my father called "Charlie."

Charlton was a special athlete, a strikingly handsome youth, gifted in many ways. He truly could run and jump with the best in the world, and one of his great strengths was his particular mental preparation. About midweek before a performance, he would start his own psyching program, and most of the time, it worked. It did, however, lend itself to overpreparing and overpsyching, which can be less than ideal, as many of us witnessed with Denver's Super Bowl 48 collapse. While Peyton Manning, one of the greatest players ever to don shoulder pads, may have overprepared for that one, he surely made up for it with his Super Bowl 50 victory.

In Charlton's case, his routine included some habits that were outside the norm for most athletes, such as taking a warm shower shortly before he competed. And even with all Charlton's gifts and strengths, if he had one weakness, it was what some might call a prima-donna tendency: he could be a bit fragile mentally. If things were going well for him, they were going *really* well. If not, he could have problems competing.

On the day of this particular meet, just over an hour before Charlton's triple-jump competition, he approached my father to announce (in his British accent), "Coach, I'm not feeling well. I don't think I'll participate today."

Surely, my father couldn't believe what he heard. Thoughts running through his head must have included, "What d'you mean, you won't participate? Are you kidding? This is the national championships! I don't care how you feel. Tough it up, get your head out of your ass, and get ready to go!"

To this day, I believe that had my father challenged Charlton with those words, the fine athlete would have wilted like a cut flower in a heat wave. But my father was a master motivator. He took an unexpected approach, as he often did, to get athletes to perform at higher levels than they believed they could. This is where +BS comes in. Rather than say harsh things that a less skilled coach might say to motivate his athlete, my father led Charlton to believe that he had great empathy for him.

"I understand how you feel," he said, "and that's really a shame. But, Charlie, I'd like you to try something to see if we can get you feeling better. Go ahead and get on your sweats, because I'd like to have you just stride through a hundred yards on the football field."

"Well, OK, Coach," Charlton said, "though I don't feel at all well."

After my father again expressed sympathetic under-standing, Charlton got his sweats on, came back, and took a position on the football field's north goal line. My father took his place on the south goal line, stopwatch in hand. He gave Charlton the signal: "Come to your mark, set, and—" and waved his hand for Charlton to take off.

At that point, my father counted: "Thousand one, thousand two, thousand three, thousand four, thousand five," and *then* started his watch. When Charlton crossed the south goal line, my father dramatically stopped the watch.

After this "sickness test," Charlton came over to my father who said, "How did you feel?"

He shook his head. "Not good."

"Charlton, with you not feeling good," my father said in slow, positive, powerful tones, "you just ran a hundred in eleven flat."

Amazed, Charlton stared at the watch. "Wow, Coach! It didn't feel that fast."

An hour later, this athlete, who had thought he was too sick to participate, became the NCAA champion in the triple jump with the second-longest jump in the world that year. This happened because a leader, his coach, turned negative thoughts he had in his mind into positive thoughts.

The story I just shared with you has been duplicated not hundreds of times, not thousands of times, but millions of times throughout history: in athletics, in business, in war, and simply in life. Call it trickery if you like, or faking, fooling, or even lying. I call it +BS, and it leads people to accomplish things they never thought possible or even dreamed they could do by changing the way they think and quickly changing their negative and inferior thoughts and actions into positive and superior ones.

My father was a special guy. By my standards, he was the best father a kid could have, which is something I hope all you readers can say about your own fathers. He was a great son to his parents and an awesome husband, father, grandfather, leader, and coach. He was a patriarch. Most who knew him well simply called him "Coach." He attended high school in Roodhouse, Illinois, and went on to an outstanding career in both football and track at the University of Illinois. After his graduation from college, he entered the field of coaching, where he remained throughout his career.

My father had an amazing attitude about life. He agreed with Coach John Wooden that when you perform, you should aim not to be better than someone else, but to be all that *you* can be, to be the best *you* can be, to become the best version of yourself. He lived by that motto for himself and for all those he coached. He embraced a powerful group of words from the movie *The Legend of Bagger Vance*: "Golf is a game that cannot be won, it can only be played." He believed the same thing about life: it's a game that can't be won, only played, and played to the fullest.

To say he was a positive guy would be a drastic understatement. Over his entire career, he was a master at building confidence in the athletes he worked with. As I grew up, I witnessed and benefited from his coaching and leadership, and I give him much of the credit for the success I attained in a life journey that included All-American in high-school football, state champion and state record holder in track, All-American in college, and an NFL career. He also impacted the careers of my children—his grandchildren—with Johnny becoming an Academic All-American at the University of Illinois and Ashley winning numerous state championships in her track and cross-country career. Our eight grandchildren wear six state championship rings, a three handicap in golf, and a division one quarterback at Ball State, partially because of the legacy of positive thinking that their great-grandfather left with them.

I was immensely fortunate to have such a father, one who was a coach, leader, and guide in my life and who used the concept of +BS on me. I well remember another track event that I took part in myself, ten years before Charlton's great victory. It was the Illinois state track meet of May 1964, held at the University of Illinois track. I was one of the best low hurdlers in the state, but not *the* best. *The* best was Andy Johnson from Alton, Illinois. I had run against Andy four times in my career, and I'd never beaten him. He was simply a little faster and a little better than me.

On the morning of the meet, my father came to me with a great dose of +BS.

"John," he said with assurance, "this is your day to beat Andy." We both already knew there was a strong wind blowing directly into the runners' faces. We also knew that I was much bigger and stronger than Andy: 195 pounds to his 160.

"You know, John," my father thoughtfully said, "running into that wind today, your strength will be the deciding factor, and you're gonna beat him."

Now, that thought had never entered my mind. Yet the moment we climbed into the starting blocks, I already felt the confidence that comes from great coaching and skilled leadership. I knew I could and would win the race.

After Andy reached the first hurdle ahead of me, the rest of the race was me closing the gap hurdle by hurdle, with that beautiful wind pushing straight into our faces. I beat Andy by a couple of inches to win the state championship in the 180-yard low hurdles, setting a new state record with a time of 18.9 seconds. Had the wind been at our backs, Andy, being wind-aided, would probably have set a national record in the low eighteen seconds. Fifty-two years later, my record still stands today.

But hold on a minute. When I said that, I was using some RBS on you: that's regular bullshit. The record did hold for eleven years, until the 180 low-hurdle race was changed to the 400-meter race.

So you see, my successful performance, as well as Charlton's later one, was the result of a great leader's use of +BS on us both.

+BS and Thinking

Geoff Colvin wrote a powerful book entitled *Talent Is Overrated.* The cover asks the question "What Really Separates World-Class Performers from Everybody Else." Colvin states that the separator is grit, grind, and just plain hard work. He makes a compelling case that world-class performers work harder than everybody else. While I agree with this premise that they *do* work harder than everybody else, I think we need to ask the question, *Why* does this happen? Why do they work harder? The answer is that world-class performers in any domain: athletics, business, or elsewhere in their lives, *think* differently from everybody else. They are masters at controlling their thoughts and in using positive BS to control their minds and thought processes. Differences are what make champions, not similarities, and the biggest difference is the way they think. Certainly, world-class performers do work harder than others, but what is causing them to have this amazing work ethic is their attitude, and attitudes are formed by thinking. It's their thinking that's the separator. This ability to control our thinking can be called many things, such as mental toughness or cognitive behavior therapy (CBT), but I prefer to call it positive bullshit. And that is what we are going to explore in the remainder of this book.

To illustrate, if you put all thirty-six NFL teams on a bell-shaped curve based on their 2016 records of wins and losses, the one farthest to the right with the best record would be the New England Patriots, the 2017 Super Bowl champions. Farthest to the left, with the worst record for that year, would be the Cleveland Browns. What distinguished one from the other?

I've shared with a number of NFL teams my idea of what makes the difference between winners and losers, and not one player has disagreed with me. If you enter each team's NFL combine assessments—40-yard dash, 225-pound bench press, jingle jangle, vertical jump, and so on—on a spreadsheet, there would be no measureable difference between the Patriots and the Cleveland Browns, or between any of the teams. Plus, all these teams work extremely hard to be all that they can be.

Yet the 2016 NFL season saw a significant difference between the Patriots and the Browns, and that difference was in the way these teams thought. That year, at least, the Patriots thought differently from the Browns. Differences, not similarities, are what make champions, and the biggest difference is the way they think.

I feel so strongly that +BS is a vital part of leadership because it deals directly with the way we think: with learning and acquiring the skill to convert negative thoughts to positive thoughts quickly. What we witnessed in Super Bowl LI, the greatest comeback in super bowl history, was a team 'The New England Patriots' that never stopped thinking they could win! In order to lead ourselves to new levels of achievement and to lead others to accomplish things they never believed they could accomplish, we must change both the way *we* think and the way *they* think. The ability to change the way one thinks is a big deal. No, that's an understatement. It's a *huge* deal, and transmuting that ability is a vital part of leadership. Reflect with me for a few minutes on some **PGOWS** (powerful groups of words) on thinking:

1. To change your life, you have to change the way you think. Behind everything you do is a thought. Every behavior is motivated by a belief. Every action is prompted by an attitude. Be careful how you think. Your life is directed by your thoughts.

2. From a work by a little-known poet, Walter D. Wintle, which incidentally was a poem my father taught me when I was a young child: "If you think you are beaten, you are. If you think you dare not, you don't. If you like to win but you think you can't, it's almost certain you won't." Life's battles

don't always go to the stronger or faster man, but sooner or later, the man who wins is the one *who thinks he can*.

3. From Earl Nightingale's wonderful book *The Strangest Secret*: "Here's the key to success and the key to failure: We become what we think about. Now, let me repeat that. *We become what we think about.* Throughout all history, the great wise men and teachers, philosophers, and prophets have disagreed with one another on many things. It is only on this one point that they are in complete and unanimous agreement. Consider what Marcus Aurelius, the great Roman emperor, said: *"A man's life is what his thoughts make of it.""*

I have spent the majority of my adult life in the world of leadership, building organizations and mentoring teams and individuals to be all that they can be. While this work occurred in many places, largely it was in the corporate and athletic worlds.

In the last chapter, we saw how a successful coach and leader, my father, inspired one of his athletes to perform at the highest level by helping him think he was healthier than he might have been. Charlton thought he was sick, and he probably was. But my father got him to *think* he was strong and capable, leading him to a national championship by helping him change his thoughts. As for me, I didn't think I could beat Andy Johnson in the state track meet until my father put the thought in my head that I could and would beat him. Just that simple mention of the wind did the trick because in an instant, it gave me a new confidence that I didn't have before.

Certainly, most people view the word bullshit, as typically used, to indicate exaggeration or deception. Let's examine that thought. Here's the definition of the word "deceive," along with an example of its use: "**deceive**, verb: to mislead by false appearance or statement; to delude. *They deceived the enemy by disguising the destroyer as a freighter.*"

Now let's dig into that example. The commander of the destroyer, probably a graduate of Annapolis—which is, by the way, one of the great leadership training experiences in the world—decides that a good game plan to defeat the enemy is to camouflage his ship, thereby deceiving them. Now picture the ship's war room as the commander lays out the game plan with his officers. Next, imagine one of his officers commenting on his plan: "But, sir, wouldn't that plan to deceive the enemy by camouflaging our ship be dishonest?" What do you suppose the commander's response to that inquiry will be?

Go back now to the national championship with Charlton, my father's world-class triple jumper. Let's suppose that my father's assistant coach, Gary Wieneke, knowing what my father is about to do to convince Charlton to compete, says, "But Bob, don't you think it's unfair to trick

Charlie into winning a national championship?" What do you think my father's response would have been? The commander's mission was to win the battle with the enemy. My father's mission was to see his athlete win the event.

Author and psychologist Pete Greider, whom I consider a mentor and friend, had an article published in January of 1992 called "The Workings of a Mental Thermostat." In it, Pete describes how a track coach worked with a runner named Don Wilder who just could not break the five-minute mile:

> One day about halfway through the season, the coach asked Don to run another timed mile, saying, "I've got a feeling today's the day. Just give it your best shot." Don crossed the finish line to see the coach jumping up and down and yelling. "You did it! You broke five minutes!" He then ran to hug the surprised and happy youth, holding out the watch stopped at 4:59. The expression on Don's face told it all—total disbelief. He looked like somebody who had just won the lottery. In a meet two days later, Don ran 4:58. And from that day on, Don consistently ran the mile in less than five minutes, continuing to improve as the season went on. In the last meet of the year he ran a 4:56 mile, something that had been unthinkable for him a few weeks earlier.

This story would not be remarkable except for the fact that the coach lied to Don when he came across the finish line that day in practice. To make Don think he had broken five minutes, the coach had stopped the watch early, when in fact, Don's actual time was 5:02. Just like my father, this coach used +BS on his athlete.

What did this deception accomplish? It made Don change the way he thought about his ability. From that day on, Don saw himself as someone who could run a mile in less than five minutes. Everything he did was affected by this belief: his practices, his self-concept, how he handled bad days, and how hard he pushed himself in races.

You see, Don Wilder's coach knew one of the most important secrets in sports. He understood that what limits an athlete most is what he or she thinks is possible. He knew that if Don believed he couldn't break five minutes, he never would.

Here's where Pete made his point. It was as if Don had a thermostat in his mind about the level of performance possible for him. This performance thermostat is much like our home thermostats, which maintain the temperature at a certain level—a *comfortable* level—by automatically turning the furnace off and on. We set our performance thermostat according to what we're comfortable with, what we've done in the past, the kinds of shots we think we can make, and what coaches, parents, friends, and influential people in our lives tell us about our strengths and weaknesses. Then, like the furnaces in our houses, we stop when we've reached the setting on our mental thermostat. In Don Wilder's case, his thermostat was set at above five minutes for the mile until his coach made it possible for him to reset it. And it wasn't the coach who reset it—Don did, once he came to a new belief.

Think about it. If our performance is set at seventy and we're performing at a sixty level, we think, "Wait a minute, this is ridiculous. I'm better than this, so I'll work harder until I get my performance back up to seventy."

I find it interesting that eighteen years earlier than Pete's example, the exact same tactic Don Wilder's coach used was the one my father used on his world-class athlete to get him to compete at his best when he didn't feel well, and before that on me when I didn't think I could beat the guy who was supposedly the best hurdler in the state. What was limiting Charlton, Don Wilder, and me? It was ourselves, our own thinking. In every case, a skilled coach helped us all to reset our possibility thermostats and win.

I want to close this chapter with a prayer that's been close to my heart for years, one I've used in many speeches. A Lakota prayer, it was translated into English by a warrior of the Lakota Sioux tribe, Chief Yellow Lark, in 1887. This great chief clearly knew who the enemy was.

Oh, Great Spirit, whose voice I hear in the winds
And whose breath gives life to all the world.
Hear me! I am small and weak.
I need your strength and wisdom.

Let me walk in beauty, and make my eyes
Ever behold the red and purple sunset.
Make my hands respect the things you have made,
My ears sharp to hear your voice.
Make me wise so that I may understand
The things you have taught my people.
Let me learn the lessons you have hidden
In every leaf and rock.

I seek strength, not to be greater than my brother,
But to fight my greatest enemy, myself.
Make me always ready to come to you
With clean hands and straight eyes.
So when life fades, as the fading sunset,
My spirit will come to you without shame.

What shouts out to me, echoing the mission of this book, is the first sentence in the third stanza: "I seek strength, not to be greater than my brother, but to fight my greatest enemy, myself." Cartoonist Walt Kelly put the same understanding into in the mouth of his wise little possum Pogo: "We have met the enemy, and he is us."

It's not the opposition, it's not the other team, it's not the others in the office gunning for the promotion, it's not our brothers or sisters, it's us. We are the enemy. An enemy firmly planted between our ears and in our thoughts. As leaders of ourselves, as commanders of our battles with ourselves to be all that we can be, we must zero in on what's going on inside our own heads. What limiting thoughts will you find there if you search? What freeing thoughts can you put in their place?

CHAPTER 7

WHAT AM I PREPARED TO DO?

As we march through life's battles seeking to be all that we can be or helping others to be all that they can be, at every challenge, we must ask a double-barreled and key question: "Who is the enemy, and what am I prepared to do to win this battle?"

The Untouchables is a wonderful film starring Sean Connery as a Chicago beat cop and Kevin Costner as Eliot Ness, a renowned treasury agent charged with enforcing Prohibition on behalf of the Bureau of Alcohol, Tobacco, and Firearms and who had a passion and mission to put Al Capone behind bars. It includes a scene in which Connery asks Costner, "Do you want to get Capone?" (Al Capone was the gangster who had a lock on Chicago crime.)

Costner nods emphatically. "Yes!"

Connery then asks, "What are you prepared to do?"

And Costner says, "Anything under the law."

Pressing the agent hard, Connery comes back with: "And *then* what are you prepared to do?"

Those are two powerful questions we all have to ask ourselves once we've decided to climb the ladder to our unlived lives and our most amazing futures. That first question, "What am I prepared to do?" must be followed by another: "And *then* what am I prepared to do?"

Deciding to get better, or help those around us get better, calls for more than simply establishing a logical plan and following it. Oh sure, we'd all like to think we can use logic and follow a scientific plan to lead us to the promised land. We've already pointed out the importance of thoughts in dictating action, but that's not the whole story. Because we're human, we're emotional beings, and emotions are driven by thoughts. We have to learn how to deal with, or better yet, control our thoughts in order to manage our emotions.

Here's how performance psychologist, successful author and a man that has touched my life at the deepest level, Jim Loehr, defines mental toughness: "The ability to be at your best on command. It's about skill in controlling our emotions." That's a fairly simple statement, but how easy do you think controlling our emotions is? In order to learn to do it, we have to realize that we must first control the way we think.

Angela Duckworth has done some special things in her career. If you're not familiar with her work, Google her and listen to her TED (Technology, Entertainment and Design) talk. In her work with the prestigious Riverdale Country School in the Bronx, New York, she has compiled a set of strengths she believes are especially likely to predict life satisfaction, high achievement, and success. We're all familiar with the grade point average, or GPA. Duckworth calls the strengths she's identified the character point average, or CPA, and itemizes them on her unique GRIT scale. This research has convinced her that in predicting success, a youngster's CPA (character point average) is more important than his or her GPA. The components of the GRIT scale follow:

1. Zest
2. Grit
3. Self-control
4. Social intelligence
5. Gratitude
6. Optimism
7. Curiosity

In the 1960s, University of Pennsylvania psychiatrist Dr. Aaron T. Beck, working with depressive patients, came up with an approach he called cognitive therapy. Soon widely adopted in the mental-health disciplines, Beck's name for his approach was expanded to include the word "behavior": CBT. As a graduate student in psychology at the same university, Duckworth studied Beck's findings and later began to use what she had learned in her work with children. This is how she defines CBT: "Using the conscious mind to understand and overcome fears and self-destructive habits. Positive self-talk would be a good example of CBT. People who are successful in life can use the technique on themselves in a heartbeat."

In my teaching and leadership work, I've long used both Loehr's mental toughness definition and Duckworth's CBT definition, and I've based my concept of +BS on them as well. Here's my definition of +BS: the ability and skill to free the mind to change negative and inferior thoughts and actions to positive and superior thoughts and actions, quickly.

Negative thoughts are an emotional cancer, and every one of us has it. Fortunately, for some of us, it's in remission a lot of the time. But when negative thoughts do crop up and if we dwell on them, they spread—or, to stick with the cancer metaphor, they metastasize. And when this metastasis happens, those expanding negative thoughts kill productivity and destroy chances for success.

What can we do about negative thoughts? First, expect them to crop up, knowing you want to put that emotional cancer in remission. The treatment is a big dose of emotional chemo in the form of mental toughness, CBT, or +BS.

Think for a moment of the word *shock* as it refers to our minds. One of its definitions is "a sudden or violent disturbance of the mind, emotions, or sensibilities." When we experience or see something horrific, our minds can actually shut down, causing our bodies to shut down, too, a condition that if not properly treated can lead to death. What happens is that something so terrible is fed into our brains that our minds change our physiology, causing us major mental and physical problems. Nothing touched us. We were not physically harmed in any way. Yet the incredible power of the mind and the power of thinking in such a negative manner can lead to our deaths. If our minds have a dark side that can impact us in such negative ways, then shouldn't they be able to impact us with the same power in *positive ways*? The answer is, *they can.*

Consider what Daniel Goleman writes in his powerful book *Emotional Intelligence*:

> Much evidence testifies that people who are emotionally adept—who know and manage their own feelings well, and who read and deal effectively with other people's feelings—are at an advantage in any domain of life, whether romance and intimate relationships or picking up the unspoken rules that govern success in organizational politics. People with well-developed emotional skills are also more likely to be content and effective in their lives, mastering the habits of mind that foster their own productivity; people who cannot marshal some control over their emotional life fight inner battles that sabotage their ability for focused work and clear thought.

You can interpret this any way you like, but my experience tells me that being mentally tough isn't easy. It isn't easy to know and manage your emotions. Following a huge loss in your life, it's hard to simply rely on logic to make yourself feel better.

What does a doctor say to a terminally ill cancer patient? What does a coach tell his heavily outmanned, underdog team before they face the heavily favored team? What did General Omar Bradley say to his First US Army Infantry troops before they climbed in their landing craft to storm Omaha Beach on D-Day? What do you say to yourself to stay accountable for following through with actions you know will take you to the top?

The answer is, *anything* that gets the job done. You have to control your thinking and may have to deceive yourself about the odds or your chances to pull off the victory for you or for those you lead. You may have to camouflage your feelings, fake it till you make it, or for our purposes, become skilled at using +BS on yourself or others.

Robert Cooper is a neuroscientist, author, leader, and mentor of some of the world's top leaders, a guy I've been blessed to work with as my mentor and friend. His book *Get Out of Your Own Way*—a great read—explores the science of why we do some of the things we do and what we need to do to overcome our human reluctance to grow or get better. He defines and discusses *homeostasis*, a powerful mental force designed by nature to protect us by making us resist change. Homeostasis is what urges us to stay right where we are—a powerful inner magnet in that whenever we desire to grow or get better at something we think we want, it goes into action to keep us where we were before we came up with a new goal.

Along similar lines, Pete Greider says we have a design flaw, something we need to come to grips with anytime we hope to grow, get better, and climb higher on the ladder of success. In those situations, Greider says, we need to build an environment around us that will give us a compelling and immediate reason (CIR) to follow through.

Human beings' track records of following through with important aspects of their lives are amazingly dismal. Here are a few examples from research at Columbia University:

1. Less than 50 percent of heart-attack victims follow their doctors' recommendations for lifestyle changes.
2. Less than 10 percent of all books purchased are read past the first chapter.
3. Of a hundred people who join a health club, 10 percent never go, 25 percent have stopped going after one month, and after three months, 75 percent have stopped going.
4. 40 percent of smoke alarms have no batteries.
5. More than 50 percent of marriages end in divorce.

While we could go on, the point is—even assuming that human beings are the planet's most intelligent creatures—that we have great difficulty following through with challenges we set for ourselves aimed at improvement. The two Fs of greatness are *focus* and *follow-through*. Focus is tough. Follow-through is tougher. Pogo was right: we are definitely the enemy, and in order to win this fight with ourselves, we to have to develop new strategies around the way we think. I'm proposing here, of course, that the way to do it is improve our ability to use +BS.

To back up for a moment, we've already mentioned EBS and NBS. Most of us are pretty good at using both. But it's important to keep in mind that +BS is a dramatically different mindset and skillset from those two. The truth is, EBS and NBS *detract* from our leadership skills, while +BS can *enhance* them.

Before we go deeper into why +BS is so critical to leadership, let's turn to the dictionary to find out just what leadership means. Here's what Webster says about the word "leader": "As a position or function of a leader. A person who guides or directs a group." About "leadership," the dictionary gives us: "an act or instance of leading, guidance, or direction." Someone looking for a leader, or someone wanting to be one, thinks in terms of a journey, either making one or helping others embark on one. What greater journey can there be than life itself?

I've said before and will say it again. Great journeys require great guides! They lead us where we want to go, but even more important, they inspire and motivate us to go further than we thought we could go. So it's safe to say that a leader is a person who leads, guides, or directs. I've found that most people, when reflecting on leading, guiding, and directing, think in terms of leading, guiding, and directing *others*. While I certainly agree that an important part of leadership is leading and guiding others, being an effective leader starts with being able to lead, guide, and direct *ourselves*.

When I tell people I do a great deal of speaking, they usually ask, "Are you a motivational speaker?" Generally, my reply is "No." Instead, I say that I speak about leadership and facilitate leadership seminars applicable to *all* people. Everyone has a connection to leadership because everyone leads the most difficult person on this earth to lead—himself or herself.

Most folks see change as something they don't like, but I don't agree. We may not like change if it's likely to affect us negatively, but people love *positive* change. When asked, "Would you like to lose ten pounds, make more money, be a better spouse or parent, and get in good physical shape?" the answer is always a resounding "Yes!"

What people don't like about change is the transition from point A to point B. That part of change is painful. The greatest room in the world is the room for improvement, but you don't simply walk through the door into that room. You'll probably endure considerable pain when you step over its threshold.

A young professional woman in rehab for the alcoholism that had cost her a prestigious job was telling her troubles to a fellow patient. The new friend, hoping to console her, said, "I know it feels awful, Sue, but stay strong. Remember, whenever one door closes, another will open." Sue replied, "Yeah, but it sure can be hell in the hallway."

True leadership, whether leading ourselves or leading others, involves change, and change involves pain. How you feel about this next PGOW will determine whether you have the ability to change your life for the better. Here it is: the pain of change is greater than the pain of losing.

Let's don't kid ourselves. Homeostasis—staying the same—is a powerful force, almost as powerful as the force of gravity. The problem for most people is that from day to day, they don't believe they're losing. They're happy where they are, or at least fairly content, and they want to stay there. And yet, as I see it, they're losing. We are either green and growing or ripe and rotting. We're either busy living or busy dying. There is no staying the same.

Believing it's possible to stay the same is as ridiculous as putting a million dollars in a drawer and expecting that in five years, it will be the same million dollars you put away earlier. Over time, inflation will have eroded its value.

Change is painful, so much so that when facing a choice between the pain of change and staying where we are, most of us choose the latter, not realizing we're taking on the pain of losing. Staying where we are is tantamount to losing.

Here's an example we can all understand. Over the past several years, large hospitals have brought in new computer programs and require all their physicians to use them. Younger doctors, many of whom spent their formative years playing computer games, were adept at learning the new programs and putting them to use. Older doctors, particularly those who'd never even learned to type, found themselves struggling to keep up, and for some, the struggle was so painful they decided to take early retirement. When staying the same became impossible for the older group, they had to choose between the pain of change (learning the new program), which might be short-lived, or the permanent pain of losing their livelihood.

Tom Landry has always said that good coaching makes men do what they don't want to do so they can achieve something they've always wanted to achieve. Is there a leadership strategy or philosophy that helps us be more effective in leading ourselves or others? The answer is *yes*!

CHAPTER 8

THE RIVER OF RESISTANCE

WHY DO YOU suppose leading ourselves to achieve something we've always wanted to attain is often so very hard? Beyond that, why must leading ourselves effectively come first, before we acquire competence in leading others to achieve something they've always wanted to achieve? And third, why is +BS a vital part of this process?

The story is often told of a woman who brought her young son to Mahatma Gandhi.

"*Bapu,*" she said, "my son is addicted to sugar. He won't stop eating sweets no matter what. He reveres you, and I believe if you tell him to stop, he will. Help me, please."

"Come back with him in two weeks," Gandhi said. "Then perhaps I can help."

Frustrated, she took the boy home, but she came back in two weeks as instructed.

Gandhi then said, "Boy, eating too much sugar is bad for you. You must stop eating so many sweets."

The mother couldn't understand. "*Bapu,* why didn't you tell him that two weeks ago?"

"Mother," Gandhi said, "two weeks ago I was eating a great deal of sugar myself."

My business card carries three PGOWs, one saying: "Most people know how to live a perfect life. The problem isn't knowing. It's doing." No, it's not difficult to *know* how to lead yourself or others, but it's darned difficult to actually *do* it.

I hope you're reading this book because you'd like to get more out of life. There's surely something you want to do, something you'd like to accomplish: an amazing future, a yet unlived life you'd like to have.

I was coaching an extremely successful wealth adviser with Northwestern Mutual from New York, Pat Di Cerbo. Pat gave me a very special gift—a book by Steven Pressfield entitled *The War of Art*—not to be confused with *The Art of War,* the famous book from the fifth century BC by author Sun Tzu.

Pressfield contends that we all have two lives: one, the life we are presently living, and two, our unlived life. The latter is the life of our dreams, desires, goals, and our most amazing futures. He says that what separates those two lives is *resistance,* and he calls this the most evil force on this earth because it keeps us from using the gifts God gave us to be all that we can be. He goes into elaborate detail about how truly evil and powerful this resistance is. One of his descriptions of resistance will give you an idea of the power he attributes to this negative force:

"Resistance is insidious...Resistance will tell you any-thing to keep you from doing your work. It will perjure, fab-ricate, falsify, seduce, bully, cajole. Resistance is protean. It will assume any form, if that's what it takes to deceive you. It will reason with you like a lawyer or jam a nine-millimeter in your face like a stickup man. Resistance has no conscience. It will pledge anything to get a deal, then double-cross you as soon as your back is turned. If you take resistance at its word, you deserve everything you get. Resistance is always lying and always full of shit." Going along with the theme of our book, Pressfield could have easily said, Resistance is one massive pile of horse shit, chicken shit, or bullshit.

I just loved that thought. It touched me at a deep level. I was at Di Cerbo's estate when I first studied *The War of Art,* and one morning while walking around the property, I came upon an extraordinary bridge over a small stream that ran through his place. Believe me, this was no ordinary bridge Pat had built, but a beauti-ful stone bridge that must have cost north of six fig-ures. I kept studying this book, often reflecting on it during my walks, and one morning when I crossed Pat Di Cerbo's marvelous bridge over that stream, I decid-ed to rename the powerful force that Pressfield spoke of. I now call it the "River of Resistance."

This abstract River of Resistance stands directly in the path of our journey to reach our unlived lives. Our most amazing futures, our highest goals, and our most cherished dreams will never happen if we don't make the crossing. As leaders, we must first cross this river ourselves before we can lead others to cross it on their journeys.

Throughout history, the millions of miles that people have journeyed to find new lives, the crossing of rivers has always been an obstacle that they had to deal with. The River of Resistance that stands directly in our path to this new life is virtually impossible to cross, so it requires us to build a bridge. I have placed five specific obstacles in our river, which we must *first* face, recognize that they exist, then decide and measure exactly how much of an obstacle they are for us to overcome. Using the SAM acronym might be a good place to start in dealing with these obstacles. S - are they significant, A - are they attainable, M - are they measureable? Once this is done, we can determine which of the obstacles provide us with the biggest challenge, allowing us to focus and follow through with building our bridge.

As a professional athlete and a corporate executive, I have lived with and believed how important measurement is throughout my whole career. Everything a professional athlete does, such as practice and games, is measured, filmed, and reviewed. As Chris Tamas, head volleyball coach of the University of Illinois, said "films don't lie." It is also that way in the corporate world. *We can't manage what we can't measure.* If we want to cross the

64

River of Resistance, we need to know what is keeping us from doing so. I didn't mention this earlier in the book when I discussed it, but I hope that when you read the components of Angela Duckworth's GRIT scale, you scored yourself on each of them. Words that define and predict "life satisfaction, high achievement, and success" are *certainly* worth measuring. A 70 is a perfect score on her GRIT scale, and a 55 might warrant serious focus and follow-through to get that score raised. Keep in mind that a 99 isn't a good score if a 100 can be accomplished.

So now it's time for you to score yourself on the five obstacles in our river. Have a pen in hand as you go through these. Peyton Manning makes a powerful point at his quarterback camps that you should never watch your game films without a notepad. Remember, the palest ink is stronger than the greatest memory. I have found that many people, when assessing themselves, don't like to give themselves a perfect score of ten, as they feel that it leaves no room for improvement. I disagree with that philosophy, for tens can improve just as ones can improve, and actually tens probably can improve *a lot* more easily than ones. As long as you are on the bank of the river dealing with your current life and looking across at your unlived life, one or more of these obstacles are standing directly in your way.

Tʜᴇ Fɪᴠᴇ Oʙꜱᴛᴀᴄʟᴇꜱ ɪɴ ᴛʜᴇ Rɪᴠᴇʀ ᴏꜰ Rᴇꜱɪꜱᴛᴀɴᴄᴇ

1. Tʜᴇ Wᴀʟʀᴜꜱ

The walrus represents laziness, which could also be defined as a lack of grit or grind. Geoff Colvin's wonderful book *Talent is Overrated* includes a PGOW that should be in every locker room: "Hard work consistently beats talent, unless talent consistently works hard."

Certainly, people with great talent or potential are exciting, yet if they aren't willing to work hard, whatever talent or potential they possess will never amount to much. I call it the "Three Gs to Success": grit, grind, and glory. Casey Nickels, former University of Georgia football standout, and now a successful wealth advisor from Atlanta, says potential is French for "you ain't done shit yet." We all want the glory, but if we aren't willing to put in the grit and the grind, we have very little chance of even a glimpse of the glory.

Earlier, we talked about Angela Duckworth's GRIT scale and its importance in predicting success. I think it's fair to say that every coach, leader, or anyone involved in personal development knows and understands the importance of hard work. The left cornerstone of John Wooden's Pyramid of Success is industriousness, and the right cornerstone is enthusiasm. Those same qualities, by other names, are also the first two items on Duckworth's GRIT scale: grit and zest.

The walrus is a huge blob of inertia—a lack of work, grit, or grind—blocking your way across the River of

Resistance. Quite simply, ask yourself if you are working hard enough to be successful.

Now, score yourself on the walrus.

2. The Mermaids

Our mermaids in the River of Resistance represent temptations, which can turn into addictions. The sirens in Greek mythology, according to Homer's *Odyssey*, were "winged maidens" who, with their enchanting music and voices, lured nearby sailors to the rocky shores of their island and led the sailors to their deaths, which, of course, is an excellent example of NBS. Our sirens, or mermaids, represent temptations that have the propensity to turn into addictions, which include a number of things that can derail us from getting across the river to our unlived lives; these may include sex, drugs, alcohol, food, cell phones or anything else that causes us significant problems. My leadership development work has brought me in contact with many professional athletes and teams, including when I served six times as a main platform speaker for the NFL Rookie Symposium. Professional athletes, unfortunately, seem to join other famous people, like actors, politicians, entertainers, and other men and women of great power and wealth who seem to have propensities for problems with mermaids, which can become serious stressors in our lives. A professional athlete attending a camp at my Greyfield ranch was forking out a total of $30,000 every month: $10,000 each to three different women for three different paternity suits.

What I'm about to tell you might shock you, but it's not something that hasn't been made public, as it was already covered by ESPN. In one session at the first Rookie Symposium I attended, the players were given bananas so they could practice putting condoms on them. I'm sure this is the NFL's way of keeping players out of paternity suits. Before you pass judgment on this practice, be aware that the NFL was actually trying to help these players. Professional athletes and the others, as we discussed, are celebrities and have all kinds of people hunting them down, not just for their autographs. The average man or woman might find it difficult to understand just how powerful a temptation that can be.

After that presentation, I was talking with Peyton Manning, and I asked him what he thought about the material at the symposium. "Some of it's appropriate," he said, "and some of it isn't." Regardless of your opinion, sex has been with us since Adam and Eve, and sexual issues and problems can be devastating. With today's divorce rate above 50 percent, there's no question that such problems are a major issue in our society.

So, yes, sexual issues can represent addictions, along with mind-altering drugs, alcohol, pornography, eating disorders, and gambling; anything someone can be addicted to is a mermaid. A recovering alcoholic, asked about his drug of choice, said "More." That's a pretty good definition of addiction. And when "more" is your drug of choice, there's never enough.

I don't give myself a ten in scoring on mermaids. I, like Ghandi, love sweets. There's no question I would be better off if I eliminated them from my diet, but that may be one mermaid I keep for a while. The good news about the mermaid issue is that there are vast resources of professional help available for those who have such addictions to conquer.

Score yourself here on mermaids.

3. THE CRABS

Whenever I'm speaking and discussing the River of Resistance, the mention of crabs after mermaids often raises a chuckle in the audience. Obviously, they must be thinking about a different crab than the one I am about to discuss. The River of Resistance crabs live in the ocean and are very easy to catch; all you need is string and a chicken neck. Tie the string around the chicken neck, keep hold of the string's other end, and toss the chicken neck in a tidal creek. With luck, one crab or a couple of them will grab the chicken neck and hang on as you slowly pull in your catch.

Here's the interesting thing that's pertinent to our discussion about crabs. If you put one crab in a shallow bowl, it can easily climb out. Yet if you put a bunch of crabs in that same bowl, none of them can get out. Why? Because as one starts to climb out, the others grab him and pull him back into the bowl.

The crabs in our lives are the people who pull us back into our bowl, hindering us or not letting us achieve our dreams, goals, and most amazing futures.

Crabs can be almost anyone: parents, siblings, relatives, coaches, ministers, priests, or people we work with. The list is almost endless. Crabs usually come with one of two distinctly different mindsets. Group one just doesn't like seeing anyone else succeed. Small thinkers, they seem to relish seeing others fail. Group two is the protective crab, those who are merely trying to protect us from what *they* think is in our best interests.

My wife is a very special person. We have had a wonderful marriage for forty-nine years! She would measure highly on the GRIT scale, plus she's smart and exceptionally good with people. Often, she can answer most of the *Jeopardy* questions before the participants, and she's a sports maven regarding anything that deals with football. Yet with all of this going for her, she can be a protective crab at times. We had just seen the movie *Field of Dreams*. I loved the film and was really fired up by a character (Kevin Costner) who built a regulation baseball field in his cornfield in Iowa. I actually was so enthusiastic that upon leaving the theater, I proclaimed to Deanna, "What a great idea, it's just the wrong sport. We are going to build a football field."

Upon hearing this, she said, "What? Build a football field? We can't do that!" She simply was not as interested or excited as I was about a football field in our backyard. Because I am a ten at dealing with crabs, we have a regulation football field in our backyard.

A few years later, I had been facilitating a high ropes course in Wisconsin, and I returned home with excitement and plans to build a high ropes course at our home. Deanna was less excited about this than the football field, yet we have a wonderful ropes course at our home that has helped hundreds of people grow, deal with their fears, build confidence, understand the power of teamwork, and so on.

An excellent summation to our crab discussion would be a song that country western singer Buddy Jewell sings titled "I Want to Thank Everyone." This is the ultimate anticrab song: its theme is that Jewell wants to thank everyone in his life who ever told him no.

Score yourself on crabs.

4. THE SHARK

The shark represents an F word that poses a tremendous block to achievement of our goals and dreams, a major deterrent in crossing the River of Resistance to our unlived lives and our dreams. That F word is *fear*. Right now, set this book down, close your eyes, take a deep breath, and ask yourself this question: "What could I accomplish if I had no fear?" Keep in mind that courage is *not* the lack of fear. God put fear into our makeup to protect us. So let's complete that PGOW: "Courage is not the lack of fear. Courage is taking action in light of what you fear."

I like to think of fear as friction. Picture a piston in the cylinder of an engine. It runs smoothly when properly lubricated. Without a lubricant, the piston will get hot, overheat, expand, and actually lock up in the cylinder. The same thing is exactly what happens to us when we let fear take over. In a fearsome situation, we get nervous, tighten up, or lock up. We've all been there. To achieve something in spite of our fear, we have to be able to apply the lubricant of courage to our brains to keep them from locking up. This is easily said but difficult to do.

In order to overcome friction caused by our fear, we need to start a workout program to build our courage muscles. This is how the training works. Whenever you feel the friction of fear, you have a choice. You can back off, run, hide, and refuse to engage. If this is your choice, you've just weakened your resolve to become stronger in dealing with fear. Your other choice is to move into the fear, engage, and thereby strengthen your courage muscles. Every day of our lives, hundreds of times arise when we're confronted with the friction of fear. Today, you can start recognizing these moments and choose to move into them rather than away from them. Start with little, seemingly unimportant fear situations, and soon you'll be ready to work up to the big ones.

Let's suppose you have a fear of engaging people or talking to strangers. Every time you're with a stranger in an elevator, at a gas station, or in a grocery line, you'd like to say something, but you don't. If you then beat yourself up with a lot of negative thoughts, right there, you've weakened your courage muscles. I make a little game out of these exchanges. A gas station is a perfect place to build your courage muscles to deal with the fear of talking to strangers. As you're pumping gas, start a conversation. Ask your pump partner, "How do you like your car?" Then stay with whatever conversation follows. What has this little, seemingly meaningless conversation done? Instead of making your courage muscles atrophy further, it has built them up.

The late, great Nelson Mandela said it perfectly: "I learned that courage was not the absence of fear, but the triumph over it. I've felt fear myself more times than I can remember, but I hid it behind a mask of boldness. The brave man is not he who does not feel afraid—but he who conquers that fear." The greatest leaders understand the vital nature of being able to use +BS on oneself, as Mandela's PGOW perfectly illustrates with "I hid it behind a mask of boldness." Regarding our fears, William Shakespeare said, most eloquently, "Our doubts are traitors and make us lose the good we oft might win by fearing to attempt."

How do you act when your mind feels the friction of fear? Do you move away from fear more often than you move to engage with it? You can become courageous if you strengthen those courage muscles.

Score yourself on sharks.

5. THE LIBRARY

I'm a champion of lifelong learning. On my business card is another PGOW, a quote from the late, great Jim Rohn: "Learning is the beginning of health, wealth, future, fortune. You can multiply your life by 2, by 3, by 5, by 10 if you don't neglect to learn." Learning can happen anywhere and everywhere: during education, grade school, high school, in college, every day in life, and certainly, in the well-known school of hard knocks. Because libraries are such important institutions of learning, you may wonder why I would include them among other obstacles in the River of Resistance to living your unlived life.

To me, our lives represent a book. Yours is different from mine, of course, but I like to think of each year as a chapter with many subheadings. I got this thought from Jim Loehr, who wrote a great book, *The Power of Story*, which treats this important subject in wonderful detail. If we're fortunate, most of our chapters are positive, bringing many great experiences that we find valuable to go back to often and reread. On the other hand, we also have chapters we weren't pleased with when they happened—things we did that brought us no joy at the time nor when we recall them, possibly things we feel embarrassed or ashamed for having done.

After one of those not-so-cheerful happenings, we have three options. First, we can shove the event to the backs of our minds and pretend it never happened. Second, we can figure out what its lesson is, then continue to beat ourselves up for a bad choice or being dumb enough to let it happen. Or third, we can stay with the recollection long enough to see why it happened, learn from it, then put it away where we don't keep trying to dwell on it.

Learning from our mistakes is important, even critical, for our growth. Craig Tilley, CEO of Australia's nationwide tennis program and coach of multiple national championship teams at the University of Illinois, always said, "When you lose, don't lose the lesson." Echoing the same idea is a PGOW that world-class wealth adviser Rebecca Bast sent me recently: "We never lose. We either win, or we learn." These are both true north statements.

Here's my point. Once we've learned the lessons our mistakes or losses have taught us, we need to stow those chapters firmly in the reference shelves of our personal libraries. It's a shame that so many of us go back obsessively to rehash the negative stuff in our life experience—a major mistake.

As Travis Bradberry points out when discussing emotional intelligence, "decades of research now point to emotional intelligence as being THE critical factor that sets star performers apart from the rest of the pack. The connection is so strong that 90 percent of top performers have high emotional intelligence."

In discussing letting go of mistakes, he says,

> Emotionally intelligent people distance themselves from their mistakes, but do so without forgetting them. By keeping their mistakes at a safe distance, yet still handy enough to refer to, they are able to adapt and adjust for future success. It takes refined self-awareness to walk this tightrope between dwelling and remembering. Dwelling too long on your mistakes makes you anxious and gun shy, while forgetting about them completely makes you bound to repeat them. The key to balance lies in our ability to transform failures into nuggets of improvement. This creates the tendency to get right back up every time you fall down...

I love the phrase "transform failures into nuggets of improvement." Robert Cooper puts it so appropriately with "find fuel in failure." Again, as Tilley said, "Don't lose the lesson." Amen to that. But once that lesson has been learned, put that chapter away to be read only if present circumstances suggest the need for a reminder.

How are you at letting go of bad choices or past mistakes? Do you recognize the lessons they taught? Or are you using your personal library to reread negative stuff when you should be looking ahead to the positive?

Score yourself on the library.

Having looked now at all the possible obstacles in your personal River of Resistance, how many do you think you need to work on? You can begin to tackle them, one by one, at the same time as you begin building a bridge to get over the obstacles in our river.

CHAPTER 9

BUILDING THE BRIDGE

WITH YOUR SCORECARD from the River of Resistance in hand, you should now have a clear picture of what obstacles may be blocking you from getting across. Maybe there's just one, or maybe you need to work on several. In any case, you've made the diagnosis, so now it's time for the next steps, which hopefully contain the 2 Fs of greatness: focus and follow-through.

If you're ready now to move into your unlived life, let's build the bridge. Our bridge has two main structural beams, with four supports to tie it all together.

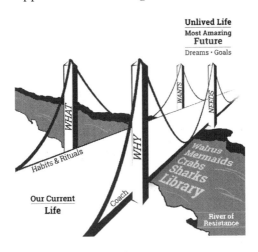

78

Let's start with habits and rituals. We are creatures of habit, a trait that's built into our being. Aristotle put it beautifully: "You can't determine your future. You *can* determine your habits and rituals. Your habits and rituals *will* determine your future. We do what we repeatedly do. Excellence then is *not* an act. It's a *habit*." We've talked before about homeostasis, which is the scientific term for this propensity to remain as we are. My iPad dictionary says this:

> **homeostasis,** noun. 1. The tendency of a system, especially the physiological system of higher animals, to maintain internal stability, owing to the coordinated response of its parts to any situation or stimulus that would tend to disturb its normal condition or function. 2. A state of psychological equilibrium obtained when tension or a drive has been reduced or eliminated.

In plain language, homeostasis is a powerful pull that wants to keep us right where we are. Robert Kennedy, an extremely bright leader, educator, and writer, has a PGOW etched on the walls of the Princeton University Student Union. It says, "Thinking that frees itself from reflective obedience to familiar sequence." What he's saying is that growth, learning, leadership—all things that certainly go on at Princeton University—need thinking that frees itself from the habits and rituals of our minds, or "reflective obedience to familiar sequence."

Stop for a second to reread that last paragraph. Why do you think there are discussions of habits and rituals on the walls at Princeton University? I'll tell you why. Because they're so important!

Let's go back to our obstacles in the River of Resistance. Let's say, as an example, that you scored yourself a five on the walrus. You believe you could have more grit and grind if you were in better physical shape. You get tired easily, and this fatigue often keeps you from following through with important things. Your habit and rituals around exercise are, simply, that you don't work out. Most people in this situation believe all they need to do is to be more disciplined and that having more discipline will get the job done, get them to work out, give them more energy, and raise their walrus score.

But this is *not* a discipline issue. It's a habit and ritual issue. Read these next words carefully: we, you and I, are 100 percent disciplined to our existing sets of habits and rituals. If you currently don't work out, you are 100 percent disciplined to that habit. When you think about working out, your habit kicks in and says to you, "Don't work out."

Now, on the flip side of this coin, let's say that you *do* work out. You have a consistent pattern of working out five days per week. So when you think about working out, your habit kicks in, and you follow through with the workout.

I'll say it again. It's not about discipline; it's about habits and rituals. If you don't work out, you are actually disciplined about *not* working out. I'll be coming back to this point after we've discussed the other parts of the bridge.

The other main beam to our bridge is a coach. We human beings have a horrible record of failing to follow through with important things. Remember the follow through statistics listed on page 56. It's just a fact; we have a hard time following through.

So the second main underpinning of your bridge is to get a coach. There's not a world-class athlete on this planet who doesn't have a coach. You might ask yourself, if they're the best in the world, why do they need a coach? It's because the best in the world have an inner drive pushing them to be *better*. And to be better, they'll need to change what they're doing. And to change what they're doing will be tough.

To report what NFL Hall of Fame football coach Tom Landry said so well: "The job of a football coach is to make men do what they don't want to do, to accomplish what they've always wanted to accomplish."

You remember my pointing out that the pain of change is greater than the pain of losing. In terms of homeostasis, it's easier to stay where we are than it is to change. Change is painful, and yet, if you are not satisfied with your current life, with the results you are getting, and with the lifestyle you have living on the south side of the

River of Resistance, and you have a desire to reach your unlived life and dreams, you are going to have to change something, and that is not going to be easy or painless. To change your existing habits and rituals or to improve your walrus, mermaid, crab, shark, and library score will take some major positive bullshit to convince your mind to go along with the change *and* the pain. To summarize, this journey of getting across the River of Resistance requires us to do something that we don't want to do in order to accomplish something we've always wanted to achieve. Great journeys require great guides who lead us to where we want to go, and more importantly, these leaders inspire and motivate us to go further than we thought we could go. In other words, guides or coaches are masters of positive bullshit. So get a coach; it's as simple as that.

We have the two main beams of our bridge completed now: habits and rituals, and getting a coach. Finally, there are four supports that will bring the whole structure together.

1. **Why.** "Why" is a very big little word. It's the reason, cause, and purpose for our doing something. And that one-word question, "Why?" needs to be answered. Crossing the River of Resistance is a big deal. It can be painful. And you won't be able to get across it unless you can answer the question: "Why am I doing this?"

2. **What.** This one is the simplest of the four supports. Most of the time, we know what to do. We all know how to live perfect lives. The problem isn't knowing, it's doing. Even though finding or discovering the "What?" is usually not difficult, it is important.

3. **Need.** Most of us need to do many things that would help us raise our lives to higher plains to accomplish whatever it is that we want. Yet most of our needs don't drive us to implement the changes to make that possible. Needs outside the realm of what's essential for life—food, water, oxygen, and so on—rarely drive us to attain them, unless they turn into our number four.

4. **Wants.** Of the four supports, this is the biggie, and it has to be a serious want. Napoleon Hill's famous book *Think and Grow Rich*, describing the six steps to goal planning. He states number one as "that state of mind known as a burning desire to win, essential to success." That want is the desire, and unless it's extremely strong, your chances of reaching your goal and of crossing the River of Resistance to your unlived life and your most amazing future or dreams are slim to none.

One last topic is important in helping you understand why crossing the river to our unlived lives is so very difficult. You now understand the concept and the power of resistance in keeping us from our unlived lives, dreams, and goals. You recognize the five entities in the river—the walrus, mermaids, crabs, sharks, and library—that stand in your way, and you've scored yourself on the ones that are your biggest challenges. We've built the bridge for you to cross the river. Now let's look at one last, very important concept that may just tie all this together. I call it "David and Goliath."

Several times now, I've mentioned my friend and mentor, Pete Greider. He has a lot of wisdom to share, and it was from him that I learned the David and Goliath concept. Pete calls it by a different name—the Wise Man and Thor—but I liked the Biblical reference, so I renamed it David and Goliath.

For those of you who aren't familiar with the Old Testament story, here's a snapshot version to set it up. When King Saul was leading the Israelite army, David was a simple shepherd lad, but he was clever and brave. His older brothers were in Saul's army, facing the might of the Philistines, and David's father sent him to Saul's forces with provisions for his brothers. Goliath, an enormous Philistine shock trooper, came out to challenge the Israelites, armored from head to toe and carrying a sword and a javelin. Goliath was a giant of a man. Picture an individual two feet taller than Shaquille O'Neal who could wear 153 pounds of armor and wield a javelin that weighed 53 pounds. And then imagine David, the shepherd boy who asked King Saul to send him out against Goliath. The only plus for David was that he was an expert with his slingshot and had often fought and killed the lions and bears who threatened his sheep. At first, Saul would have nothing to do with sending David out to face Goliath. But David's persistence finally won out, and Saul agreed to the battle between David and Goliath. Saul gave David his own armor to use in the battle, but David, unaccustomed to such encumbrances, laid it aside, taking only his staff, sling, and pouch with five smooth stones. When David approached Goliath, the giant laughed and mocked him. David, paying no attention to Goliath's mocks, took aim with his slingshot and hit Goliath in the head with a stone, knocking him to the ground. He then seized Goliath's sword and cut off his head, carrying it back to Saul as proof of his victory.

So how does this story apply to us? Our minds have two extremely important yet vastly different thought processes going on all the time. Think of it as having both a David and a Goliath because, believe me, we all have both of them helping or hindering us every day of our lives. David represents wisdom. (I fully realize the biblical David had his ups and downs, but certainly he ended on the right note.) Our David knows right from wrong and is extremely wise in all things, yet he has has no power. The David of the story didn't kill Goliath because he was stronger than him. He killed him because he was smarter than him. In our case, we actually don't want our David to kill our Goliath; we just want him to learn to control our Goliath. We already have David's moral compass and wisdom; now we want to use our Goliath's great strength to help us grow.

So what are the traits of our Goliath? He certainly isn't the sharpest pencil in the box. He isn't very smart but has tremendous strength, and he demonstrates five very predictable behaviors:

1. He conserves energy.
2. He seeks pleasure.
3. He avoids pain.
4. He embraces fear.
5. He resists change.

This last trait of our Goliath, resisting change, connects to the first four and affects our behavior regarding them in both positive and negative ways.

Go back now to our discussion of homeostasis. Goliath is going to do everything in his power—and remember just how much power he has—to keep us exactly where we are. Let's measure Goliath's traits in regard to the River of Resistance entities, keeping clearly in mind that Goliath's preponderant trait is resisting change. So how does he help or hinder us with the obstacles in the river?

He conserves energy. The walrus is about grit and grind or lack thereof. We are 100 percent disciplined to our existing set of habits and rituals because our Goliath doesn't want to change. Goliath will exert his tremendous power to keep us exactly where we are with all our habits, whether good or bad, healthful or not.

Suppose you scored yourself high on grit. You see yourself as a grinder. In that case, your Goliath will use all his strength and power to help you continue down that path. Yet if you consider this an area of your life that you need to improve, and you feel that you need to work harder and exhibit more grit and grind in your life performance, then your Goliath will use his power and strength to keep you right where you are and not become the worker bee that you desire to be.

Let's use exercise as an example. You are a fitness maven. You work out five days per week and are in outstanding shape. Your body fat is at 16 percent. You look and feel great. Once these habits and rituals are established, it's your Goliath that keeps you on the straight and narrow. On those days when you just don't want to work out, it's your Goliath that makes you follow through.

Then on the flip side of the exercise coin, let's say that you don't work out at all. Your body fat is 35 percent. You are, by definition, obese. You tire easily and lack the energy you need to be all that you can be.

Then you read an article promoting the attributes of being in good physical shape. Your David gets excited about turning over a new leaf in terms of fitness, but it's your Goliath that will exert all his power and strength to keep you right where you are. Goliath is basically Pressfield's resistance.

Just as our exercise maven is 100 percent disciplined to her set of habits and rituals and has her Goliath keeping her following through, our nonexerciser is 100 percent disciplined to her habit of not exercising, and her Goliath will keep her there.

Yet in reading this, you start to feel that it certainly makes good sense to get on an exercise program. That's your David talking to you. He says, "If you're in shape physically, you'll have a dramatically better life in all its aspects." Think of it this way: we are 100 percent disciplined to our existing set of habits and rituals because our Goliath, regardless if it's the right path or the wrong path, good or bad, will keep you there.

This same rationale applies to all the obstacles in the river. Whether you score yourself high or low, it's your Goliath that's largely responsible for your performance, good or bad. So now you're saying, "OK, I understand this, but how does one get Goliath to change and support and guide positive habits and rituals?"

Greider would say that our Goliath needs a CIR (compelling and immediate reason) to change. Our Goliath does not like pain, so the trick is to use our David's slingshot, not to kill Goliath, but to cause our Goliath pain. Giving our Goliath a consistent and strong enough CIR will often be enough to turn him to the positive side of new habits and rituals that help us grow and prosper versus holding us to the habits and rituals that inhibit our growth. If you care to dig deep into this critically important subject, I suggest you get *Following Through* by Pete Greider and Steve Levinson. It's a book to read first, then study. One final thought regarding our David and Goliath: because Goliath is not very smart, he is susceptible to being tricked, fooled, or motivated through the use of +BS. The stories I have shared are examples of great coaches (leaders) motivating their athletes with the use of +BS in changing their mindsets from negative thinking to positive thinking quickly.

THE FIVE CS OF LEADERSHIP

As we continue to think about leadership, both leading ourselves and others, I want to have you complete one more leadership assessment.

As I said earlier, we own three horses: Cisco, Red, and Tyler. None of our horses have a brand on them. But if I were to brand them, or if I would have a brand for our "ranch," it would be what I would call the five Cs brand.

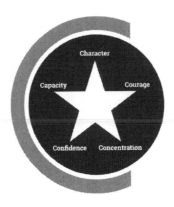

As we discuss the 5 Cs of leadership, assess how you measure up on each of them. Once again, it might be valuable to score yourself using a one through ten scale. If you feel you are in command of one of the Cs, score yourself high: eight, nine, or ten. To repeat what we have said earlier (remember that repetition is the mother of learning), one can't manage what he or she can't measure.

None of us can become a better or more effective leader without first measuring our leadership skills and then taking action to improve them.

The large C that surrounds the 5 Cs in the star is the C of greatness, which is *consistency*. Most of us, at times in our lives, have touched greatness. We can have moments of outstanding character, courage, concentration, confidence, and capacity. What separates the best from the rest is consistency. The *best* have strong traits of character, courage, concentration, confidence, and capacity *most* of the time, not once in a while. Score yourself on where you stand regarding the 5 Cs of leadership.

1. Character. If you have a strong desire to lead, especially to lead others, I consider it crucial for you to score high in character. It's certainly important for leaders to have a moral compass. Society loves men and women who are "good" people who adhere to the Ten Commandments, who live the Boy or Girl Scout code, and so on. And I respect and honor all those attributes, also. Yet, as important as all those things are, they are not what I want you to measure yourself on regarding your character. As we all know, throughout history, there have been leaders who were strong, effective leaders but unfortunately lacking when it came to the type of character I just described. Rather, I'd like you to ask yourself and measure yourself on "do you walk your talk?"

Think how hard it is to follow someone who says one thing and does another, someone with no alignment between words and actions. Think about a leader in your life: a parent, teacher, coach, mentor, or business executive who *didn't* walk their talk. These people are *very* difficult to follow.

Great leaders throughout history have been men and women who led from the front. Leading from the front is doing what you say you're doing. So now score yourself on walking your talk: with yourself, your spouse, your children, and others you lead in your business or professional life.

2. Courage. A person with courage is someone we respect. Honor, a wonderful word, attaches to those who exhibit courage. Following a courageous person is easy, but keep in mind that courage is not the same thing as lack of fear. Courage is taking action in light of what you fear. If you let it, fear can cause friction (which was our shark discussion on page 71) that will paralyze you and keep you from tapping into your courage.

During my many years of speaking to audiences of professional athletes, I often used my Water Bottle Courage Drill to show these players how the friction of fear affects us. I would pick a volunteer from the team to come up front, and I would hand him a water bottle and tell him to flip it a full 360-degree rotation while imagining that the cap was sharp enough to cut his hand severely if he missed. These were professional athletes, so they rarely had a problem with this little drill, and they certainly didn't feel the friction of fear.

Then, to make it a bit more difficult, I had them flip it two full rotations, usually with the same result—no friction of fear. At that point, I'd then say to the audience, "Well, this isn't working. We're just not seeing the friction of fear."

So I then would reach into my briefcase and pull out a big, bad-looking bowie knife, one with a twelve-inch, razor-sharp blade. And to highlight the blade's sharpness, I'd hold up a piece of paper and, with one easy pass, cut it in half.

I would then hand my volunteer the knife and ask, "Do you want to start with one full rotation or two?" Believe me, the player and the audience then saw and felt the friction of fear. Of course, I never let a player throw the knife because a miss would mean we'd need the trainer to stitch up his hand.

I'll never forget doing this with the Baltimore Ravens when Michael Oher was a rookie. I used Michael as my volunteer, and when I handed him the knife and asked him, "Do you want to try one rotation or two?" he looked me right in the eye and said, "You do it first, then I will." When I quickly did a successful double rotation and handed the knife back to him, his teammates enjoyed a big laugh. Without question, had I let him, Michael would have flipped the knife.

So now score yourself on courage. When faced with the friction of fear, do you go into the fear, or do you back away from it? Remember, going into the friction of fear strengthens your courage muscles; backing away from it weakens them.

3. Concentration. Concentration is probably the best definition of the overused but quite powerful word *focus*. Most people, even those with average levels of talent, can be very effective when they truly focus on something. I once heard that Warren Buffett and Bill Gates were in a meeting where the facilitator asked them to write down the *one* word most responsible for their success. Both, not knowing what the other was going to say, wrote down the word *focus*. Yes, it's that important.

I have a world-class shotgun shooting range at Greyfield, where I teach shooting for the dual benefits of fun and learning. The key to firing a shotgun at a moving target effectively (with accuracy) is to focus on the target, not the barrel of the gun. When we focus on the target, we have the greatest chance to hit the clay pigeon. When we look at the barrel, we will miss the target.

Most people have a lot of gun-barrel viewing in their lives. Gary Keller's *The One Thing* is a great book, a must read. In it, he declares that "multitasking" is a lie; in other words, it's NBS, or negative bullshit. Yet for many people today, what they call multitasking is the rule, not the exception: being on the cell phone while driving, being on the cell phone while eating dinner with the family, and so on. Texting while driving, yes, which I have been guilty of doing, is not only scary, but stupid. Do you believe these "multitaskers" are doing any of their multiple activities effectively? Is this something you find yourself doing?

Great leaders are great listeners. They are aware of what people say and what is going on around them. David Marquet, Captain, US Navy (retired) who was the skipper of a nuclear submarine, wrote an excellent leadership book, *Turn the Ship Around!* He uses an acronym, which he calls S.O.S., that is an excellent reminder of how to listen more effectively: S = stop what you are doing, O = open your ears, and S = show you understand.

For someone who seeks to be a good leader, focus is amazingly effective in bringing leadership about, provided the would-be leader simply focuses on whatever he or she wants to accomplish. Almost anyone, if he or she truly focuses on what it is he or she wants to do, can be successful. Score yourself on your ability to concentrate and to focus exclusively on the task at hand.

4. Confidence. I can come very close to accurately determining a person's confidence by just watching that person walk into a room. Confidence radiates throughout a person's entire being. Without confidence, no athlete, professional, or person in any walk of life can be effective. Confidence is a crucial ingredient for success and certainly a crucial ingredient for leadership. Helen Keller said it so well: "Optimism is the faith that leads to achievement. Nothing of significance can be accomplished without hope and confidence." We develop and build our confidence through successes.

I'm big on building confidence by little personal victories every day. Eric Butorac, professional tennis player, said in a TED talk, "Dream small because you might just *win* big." I get excited when I do little things well or correctly, and I celebrate them with a high five by myself. If I drop the soap while showering and make a great catch before it hits the shower floor, I get so excited I may spike the soap. Build your own confidence by getting excited about little victories, the ones no one can keep you from having. Little victories can build big confidence, and big confidence will lead to big victories. Score yourself on confidence.

5. Capacity. Capacity is *energy*, and energy is life itself. Scott Weiss, chairman of Speakeasy, a top-notch leadership organization, says great leaders need three things to connect with the people they lead: authority, *energy*, and awareness. There's no question that if you're lacking in energy, you'll find it very difficult to lead yourself, much less anybody else. Vince Lombardi said, "Fatigue makes cowards of us all." What a powerful and true statement! Do you think an exhausted or cowardly leader can be effective? Of course not.

Jim Loehr's energy pyramid has four energy domains.

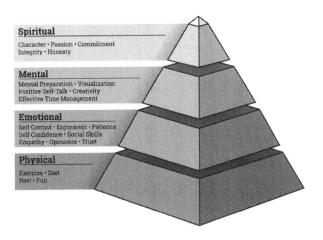

Its foundation is physical energy, followed by emotional energy, mental energy, and, finally, spiritual energy. All four are important, and they need to be in balance. It's impossible to lead if you don't have the capacity to lead, and you won't have the capacity to lead if you lack the energy to lead. Score yourself on capacity.

You have now read, hopefully reflected upon, thought about, and measured yourself as to where you stand with regard to the obstacles in the River of Resistance (walrus, mermaids, crabs, sharks, and library) and the five Cs of leadership (character, courage, concentration, confidence, and capacity). Stephen Covey's second habit in his life-changing book, *The 7 Habits of Highly Effective People*, is to begin with the end in mind, which is about goal planning. It's about seeing and creating something in your mind first and then creating it in reality. It's about thinking about crossing the river. It's about thinking about being a better leader. So, in your mind now, you know where you stand in getting across the river and the five Cs. To improve your score and to be a better leader, you are going to have to change something about the way you do things, and that starts with improving the way you think. There are many ways to improve our thinking. We send our children to school to improve the way they think. We go to college to improve the way we think. This might be an oversimplification, but generally speaking, positive thoughts produce positive results, and negative thinking produces negative results. I've already said this in earlier chapters, but it's definitely worth repeating. To change our lives, we need to change the ways we *think*. Behind everything you do is a *thought*. Every behavior is motivated by a *belief*. Every action is prompted by an *attitude*. Be careful *how* you think. Your life is directed by your *thoughts*. If our lives are what our thoughts make of them, it certainly benefits us to make sure our thoughts are helping us as much as they can. Many times, our minds just don't want to do what is best for us. Often, we flat out don't want to be our best. We feel lazy; we don't want to engage others. We don't want to get up for the big game or big appointment. Great competitors know and understand this, and they get ready to be *in* the game by using mental toughness or CBT to get ready. Both of those are perfect examples of *positive bullshit*.

CHAPTER 10

CONCLUSION
MAKING THE CASE

BULLSHIT—A GOOD WORD and A Vital Part of Leadership.
I'm sure what probably went through your mind when
you first picked up this book was that even though
you'd never given it much thought, bullshit is indeed a
good word. But then, the second part of the title, *A Vital
Part of Leadership,* might have been a bit more difficult
to accept.

After having a little fun in the beginning, in the last
five chapters, we've spent some serious time talking about
you and your ability to lead yourself and others. We looked
at a very successful Division One head track coach who
worked on the mind of a world-class athlete to get him to
win an NCAA championship. We saw how that same coach
adjusted my thinking to help me win a state championship. We read Pete Greider's story of yet another coach
getting his athlete to think differently so he could break
the five-minute mile.

We discussed at length the River of Resistance and the obstacles in it that keep us from our unlived lives, and I gave you time to score yourself on each one. We discussed how habits and rituals and having a coach are essential in building a bridge over the River of Resistance. Last of all, we reviewed the five Cs of leadership with another opportunity for self-evaluation.

So now I want to ask you: Are you seriously buying into my belief that +BS—positive bullshit—is a vital part of leadership?

I'd like for you to think of yourself sitting on a jury as you listen to me make a case for my belief. When I make this claim, I'm certainly not trying to pass off some sort of fraud on the readers of this book. What I've said about +BS being a vital part of leadership is something I believe in deeply as a true north principle.

My wife Deanna and I have been married for forty-nine years. She has a special love for movie and television courtroom dramas. At one time or another, I think she's watched every episode of *Matlock*. Since we're together a great deal of the time, I've seen many of these programs myself, or at least parts of them.

Not long ago, we saw the movie *Woman in Gold* starring Helen Mirren and Ryan Reynolds. Mirren played the daughter of a Jewish family living in Austria during World War II whose home was razed by the Nazis and had priceless personal treasures stolen. One of those treasures was a special and, in fact, famous painting by Gustav Klimt of the woman's aunt in a golden dress, giving the movie its title. This gripping and true story had Mirren hire a young, rather inexperienced attorney, played by Reynolds, to plead her case to get the picture back. It ended well, as they recovered the painting, worth in excess of $150 million.

With that inspiration, I ask you now to draw on your imagination to visualize me, the author of this book, being charged with fraud because of my belief that +BS is a vital part of leadership. Since this is an imaginary scene, picture me presenting my case in a trial complete with judge and jury. So now, let the trial begin.

Your Honor, I'd like to start my defense by asking your forbearance as I present my qualifications as an expert in leadership. I have spent the majority of my professional life helping men and women become more effective in leading both themselves and others.

Following my NFL career, my leadership experience has fallen into two separate roles. The first, which I pursued for twenty-seven years, was as the managing partner—a position akin to CEO—of Northwestern Mutual's Regional Office in central Illinois, located in Champaign. Northwestern Mutual has seventy-two regional offices throughout the country, most of them in large metropolitan cities, including New York,

Philadelphia, Pittsburgh, Charlotte, Atlanta, Miami, New Orleans, Dallas, Chicago, Nashville, San Francisco, and Los Angeles, to name a few.

Of course, Champaign, with its population of eighty thousand, is significantly smaller than the other cities I've mentioned, and if not the smallest one incorporating a network office, it is at least one of the smallest. In that limited marketplace, I recruited, trained, and developed enough field leaders—new managing partners—to put me among the top developers of leaders in the history of this great company. Because of my record, I am now asked to speak on leadership and the development of leaders on a regular basis throughout the country.

My second role, which I have focused on for the last fourteen years, is running leadership camps at our eighty-acre estate called Greyfield. I took its name from the famous Greyfield Inn on Cumberland Island off the Georgia coast. At one time, the whole of Cumberland Island, a magnificent twenty-five-mile-long piece of world-class real estate, belonged to Andrew and Thomas Carnegie. Even today, this property, which includes perfectly preserved mansions of the Carnegies and famous ruins of other mansions, offers memories and lessons from the greatness of the Carnegie brothers. Both the island and the inn are historic masterpieces, wonderful bucket-list items for anyone who can visit.

One of Andrew Carnegie's great gifts to the leadership world was his Master Mind principle. After journalist Napoleon Hill publicized this principle in his book *Think and Grow Rich,* Master Mind groups of men or women began to come together to share thoughts, experiences, dreams, and goals, both to help them become better people and to help improve the group as a whole.

Before I came up with the idea of establishing and running these leadership camps, I spent twenty-plus years in a Master Mind group myself, including some of the best men with the best minds in the wealth-advisory business. These men provided invaluable advice and training for my own wealth-advisory career and helped mold me into the leader that I am today. I am forever grateful to this group of special men, which includes Peter Hearst, Bob Pogue, Bill Goodwin, Don Romero, Phil Pierz, Tom Richards, and Tom O'Brian. Every January over this twenty-year span, our Master Mind group traveled to Cumberland Island to stay at the Greyfield Inn.

While the name *Greyfield* came from my experiences on Cumberland, the inspiration to create these leadership camps arose from my experiences at the annual NFL Rookie Symposium. From 1996 through 2001, I was a main platform speaker at these events, and while I have many wonderful memories from those times with the drafted rookies, I was also troubled by some of the things I saw there. It's no secret that the track records of many NFL players after they leave the game is far from stellar. A high percentage end up broke soon after their retirement from the NFL, and many seem to attract a lot of problems besides financial ones.

Being so close to these rookies led me to the thought that many of them lacked the life skills that would be helpful following their athletic careers as they transitioned from the NFL to the real world. Our first leadership camp was the combined brainchild of Dwayne "D.J." Joseph, then player development coach of the Chicago Bears, and myself. He and I were totally aligned in our concerns for these players, and I'm eternally grateful to D.J. for arranging my meeting with Jerry Angelo, then the Chicago Bears' general manager, to see if we could create a camp for the Bears' rookie class of 2003.

It was a meeting I will never forget. The whole thing lasted about ten minutes. After I explained what I had in mind, Jerry asked me just one question. "Why do you want to do this?"

"I don't really know," I told him. "All I do know is that something really good will come of it." He didn't say anything for thirty seconds, and I didn't say anything, so we both sat there, totally silent. Believe me, thirty seconds is one heck of a long time to say nothing. Then Jerry said, "I think your heart's in the right place. We will do this."

So our first leadership camp was born. We decided to include all of the Bears' newly drafted players for 2003. When I say that this camp was an amazing success, I'm making a gross understatement. All twelve of those draft choices made the team that year, becoming a group headed by Lance Briggs and Charles "Peanut" Tillman, who both went on to win multiple All-Pro designations, with Tillman becoming NFL's Man of the Year for 2013. We repeated the camp the following year for the Bears' drafted rookies of 2004. I believe that, without question, those two classes, along with what they learned at our camps, were vitally important in taking the Bears to the Super Bowl in 2005.

Word of the success of those camps quickly spread to the business world, and we've been holding camps like the first two we put together for the Bears ever since. The roster of our campers would make an impressive list of who's who in the athletic and business worlds.

Our Greyfield property of eighty acres includes plenty of fun facilities to help our campers focus on the real reason they come, which is to change their lives and to change the way they think. The fun areas include two fishing ponds, one of ten acres and another of one; a nine-hole par-three golf course; a "Field of Dreams" regulation football field; a world-class sporting clay shooting facility; a high ropes course; a tennis court; a riding stable; and a dog kennel.

The camps accommodate eight participants. Around sixty days before a camp, we send the prospective campers a letter to help them prepare mentally and, possibly, physically to attend. The following is a typical example of a precamp letter.

Dear Camper,

Sixty days from today, you will be at Greyfield. Our team is looking forward to seeing you and making this a most memorable experience, possibly a "live over" experience that you can reflect on for the rest of your life. Our time together will be a balance between *stress* and *recovery*. The stress will be learning and growing. We are going to school, and the subject is *you*. The recovery will be play. My life of teaching and coaching has taught me that focus follows fun. We will do both "*full go*" with the attitude of being *in* the game, not just *at* the game.

Everyone attending our camp is in a leadership position. You may have demanding positions leading your company, office, practice, team, staff, and so on. But regardless, you definitely lead the most difficult person in the world to lead: *yourself.*

The daily treadmill that we are on to obtain a life of personal satisfaction, high achievement, and success keeps us going at warp speed and doesn't seem to ever stop to let us meditate, think, plan, or envision where we have been in the past, where we are in the present, and where we are going in the future. Your time at Greyfield gets us off that treadmill for forty-eight hours.

We often hear from our campers after their time at Greyfield. I have included comments from three different business professionals who recently attended one of our camps.

Camper 1
John,

Thank you so much for our time at Greyfield. It could not have been more timely. I have been personally thinking of many of the themes we discussed as I take stock of my life. Your lessons put what I was feeling in perspective. I am already using and implementing strategies learned there.

Camper 2
John,

Well, that was certainly an experience I'll remember for the rest of my life. The setting, the company, the self-discovery, leadership training—you were right, it was a balance between stress and recovery. Just like *life* is. I can't thank you enough—Deanna, Robin, your staff, Bear, everyone—for making it a *special* weekend.

I thought much about the River of Resistance in my life and the obstacles that exist. I've taken away so many mental toughness exercises that will help me overcome them.

Camper 3

John,

We don't quite know how to even begin to say thank you. Our forty-eight hours spent with you were the most impactful, inspiring, motivating hours of our lives. The knowledge shared and advice given will stay with us forever.

Your Honor, thank you for giving me the time to review my leadership history. My sole purpose was to make a case that I do have experience in leadership that lends itself to expert testimony in terms of my credentials of recognizing, teaching, and fostering leadership skills in the people with whom I am blessed to work.

I trust that all I have said in this book until now makes it clear that leadership deals with change. If we go to Merriam-Webster's dictionary and look up "lead," we'll find a column two inches wide and eight inches long containing roughly 420 words to describe this multifaceted word, which can mean many different things.

I find that the most successful people I work with have obsessions with improvement. They have strong drives to be better. They want to continue to climb to higher ground. They fear failure, but it doesn't paralyze or freeze them into inertia. Rather, it drives them. It is a strength, not a weakness.

They are powerful leaders of others, not because of what they say, but what they *do*. They lead themselves first, they walk their talk, and others follow. This obsession to get better, to change where they are, requires difficult work. It's not a trait found in the average person, which is why the average person is average. Differences, not similarities, are what make champions, and the biggest difference is in how they think. If the way one thinks isn't doing the job, then it's time to change those thoughts.

The ability to control one's thoughts is a rare and special talent. Successful people know this, and they know they can control their thinking. They know that having this skill helps them cross the line from good to great, from success to significance. I believe there are millions of people who haven't cultivated this ability simply because they don't understand the concept of controlling their minds. They don't understand that they too can control their thoughts, which is the foundation and starting point to controlling their lives.

Let me ask you, Your Honor and men and women of the jury, is it wrong to help change a person's mind from a negative to a positive state? Is it wrong to change a losing performance to a winning performance by putting something helpful in the performers' minds? If we can learn to eliminate or reduce negative thoughts and turn them into positive thoughts, by learning to use the techniques of mental toughness, CBT, or +BS, shouldn't we be going full speed ahead to master those techniques?

From the first words of this book, I have contended that bullshit is a good word and a vital part of leadership. It's about getting ourselves and others to climb the mountain; to cross the River of Resistance; to improve and grow; and to be green and growing, not ripe and rotting. At its core, leadership of ourselves and others is about *changing the way we think.*

If we desire to become better leaders of ourselves and others, we must start thinking differently. Positive bullshit, +BS, is how we begin the process. This is nothing more than *mental makeup.* The world we live in is full of things we use every day to help us think better or feel better about ourselves. Deodorant makes us smell better. Toothpaste makes our breath better. Makeup makes us look better, as does plastic surgery. Our clothes help us look the way we want to look. Wigs or hair transplants give us the hair we don't have naturally. I could continue with page after page of things we do to feel better about ourselves, all of which are camouflaging our real selves. The question I ask is, are those things fraudulent? Is it wrong to use them? I feel the answer to those questions is a resounding *no!* Positive bullshit is nothing more than mental or emotional makeup. The reason positive bullshit is a vital part of leadership is that it makes us feel better, and when we feel better, we think better; most importantly, when we think better, we *do* better.

In conclusion, I believe that +BS is an art, a trade, a quality, and a skill that some of the greatest leaders of our time use as a powerful motivational, inspirational, and even comforting tool. Good leaders and coaches motivate their players and teams to achieve to their potential; great leaders and coaches motivate their players and teams to achieve *beyond* their potential.

Few humans recognize and respect the power our minds have over us! Reflect back to our discussion of shock and the fact that our minds can actually cause us to *die* by and through enough negative thinking. So is there an upside to the power of our minds? Absolutely. Orison Marden, an American inspirational author who wrote about achieving success in life and founded *SUCCESS* magazine in 1897, put it so well: "Deep within humans dwell those slumbering powers; powers that would astonish them, that he never dreamed of possessing; forces that would revolutionize his life if aroused and put into action."

Isn't it time that *we* awaken the amazing powers we have, though we don't even realize or recognize that we have them? Powers that would *astonish* us as to how *great* we *can* be.

If we become what we think about, it's time we start thinking about the right stuff. +BS is a vital part of leadership because it simply helps us *think better.*

It has been a total joy, Your Honor and men and women of the jury, to present my case to you. Throughout my many years of fostering leaders, I have always adhered to the PGOW that "when you believe, you are believed." I hope it is clear how much I believe in what I have shared with you.

Live a life uncommon. Now is your time.

Strength and Honor,

John Wright

Acknowledgements

I HAVE ACCOMPLISHED very few things in my life and in this world completely by myself. Writing this book echoes that statement, as so many people helped me transform my author's dream into reality.

I want to express my gratitude and heartfelt thanks to....

My mother and father, Robert and Mary Wright, who raised and led me to become the man and leader that I am.

My wife Deanna, whose steadfast support and amazing ability to see things that I don't, is so helpful to me.

My son Johnny, who relentlessly pushed and supported me to get this project done.

My daughter Ashley, whose belief in me and enthusiasm for all that I do is such a motivator.

The rest of my family, daughter-in-law Laura, son-in-law Mark, and grandchildren Julia, Joanna, Maclane, Faith, John, Caroline, Elle, and Wright, for their questions, comments, and support.

Professional authors and editors Justin Spizman and Betsy White, who contributed so much to this entire effort.

Dave Krueger, M.D., author, executive mentor coach, whose knowledge of how to get a project like this completed was invaluable to me.

Pete Greider, M.Ed., a mentor of mine, who co-authored the critically-acclaimed book *Following Through*, helped me to follow through with this book.

Keith Wagner and Scott Hodgkins, who read and critiqued manuscripts, providing what I call the "breakfast of champions" feedback.

Sherre Lucas, one of my wife's closest friends, who made the comment during a drive from Scottsdale to Tucson, that writing this book was a "good idea."

Megan Learned, my amazing team member, who is so good at getting things done, and getting them done correctly.

And, a special thank you to everyone who encouraged and supported me throughout this project.

NOTES

3. THE ORIGINS OF BULLSHIT

16 *one of the most popular swear/cuss/curse words/profanities.* Description from *Urban Dictionary*, s.v. "shit," accessed August 24, 2017, www.urbandictionary.com/define.php?term=shit.

17 *tofu of cursing and can be molded to whichever condition the speaker desires.* Quote from David Sedaris, *When You Are Engulfed in Flames* (New York, NY: Little Brown and Company, 2008), 56.

5. A NATIONAL CHAMPIONSHIP

37 *cannot be won, it can only be played.* Dialogue from the film *The Legend of Bagger Vance*, Robert Redford, director. DreamWorks, 2000.

6. +BS AND THINKING

40 *grit, grind, and just plain hard work.* Quote from Geoff Colvin, *Talent is Overrated: What Really Separates World-Class Performers from Everybody Else* (New York, NY: Penguin Group, 2008).

42 *If you think you are beaten, you are. If you think you dare not, you don't.* Quote from Walter D. Wintle, "Thinking," Unity Track Society, Unity School of Christianity (1905) accessed August 2017, allpoetry. com/poem/8624439-Thinking-by-Walter-D-Wintle.

43 *the key to success and the key to failure: We become what we think about.* Quote from Earl Nightingale, *The Strangest Secret: How to Live the Life You Desire* (Naperville, IL: Simple Truths, LLC, 2005), 29.

44 *the word "deceive," along with an example of its use.* Definition and example from *Dictionary.com*, accessed July 31, 2017, http://www.dictionary.com/browse/deceive?s=t.

7. What am I Prepared to Do?

52 *the character point average, or CPA.* Quote from Angela Duckworth, *GRIT: The Power and Passion of Perseverance* (New York, NY: Scibner, 2016).

53 *Using the conscious mind to understand and overcome fears and self-destructive habits.* Paul Tough, "What if the Secret to Success is Failure?" *The New York Times Magazine*, The Education Issue, September 14, 2011, accessed August 2017. www.nytimes.com/2011/09/18/magazine/what-if-the-secret-to-success-is-failure.html.

57 *what Webster says about the word "leader."* Definition from *Webster's New World Dictionary of American Language*, College Edition (The World Publishing Company, 1964).

8. The River of Resistance

63 *Resistance will tell you anything to keep you from doing your work.* Quote from Steven Pressfield, *The War of Art: Break*

Through the Blocks and Win Your Inner Creative Battles (New York, NY: Warner Books, 2002), 9.

66 *Hard work consistently beats talent, unless talent consistently works hard.* Quoting Geoff Colvin, *Talent is Overrated: What Really Separates World-Class Performers from Everybody Else* (New York, NY: Penguin Group, 2008).

76 *emotional intelligence as being THE critical factor that sets star performers apart from the rest of the pack.* Quoting Travis Bradberry, "Take the Test: Access the #1 Measure of Emotional Intelligence (EQ)" (TalentSmart: World's #1 Provider of Emotional Intelligence). www.talentsmart.com/test, accessed March 23, 2015.

9. BUILDING THE BRIDGE

83 *a burning desire to win, essential to success.* Quoting Napoleon Hill, *Think and Grow Rich* (New York, NY: Fawcett Books, 1960), 35.

94 *a lie; in other words, it's NBS, or negative bullshit.* Quoting Gary Keller with Jay Papasan, *The ONE Thing: The Surprisingly Simple Truth Behind Extraordinary Results* (Austin, TX: Bard Press, 2012).

94 *an excellent reminder of how to listen better.* Quoting L. David Marquet, *Turn the Ship Around! A True Story of Turning Followers into Leaders* (New York, NY: Penguin Group, 2012).

95 *Dream small because you might just win big.* Quoting Eric Butorac, "Don't Dream Big," TEDx video, 12:41, posted May 2017, baseline.tennis.com/article/66156/eric-butorac-gives-ted-talk-about-dreaming-small.

10. MAKING THE CASE

111 *powers that would astonish them.* Except from "Orison Swett Marden Quotes," AZ Quotes, www.azquotes.com/author/9452-Orison-Swett-Marden. Accessed August 24, 2017.

Made in the USA
Coppell, TX
05 February 2021